CHRISTIAN ADVENTURES

BEN-HUR
THE PILGRIM'S PROGRESS
ROBINSON CRUSOE
THE SWISS FAMILY ROBINSON

BARBOUR
PUBLISHING, INC.
Uhrichsville, Ohio

© 2001 by Barbour Publishing, Inc.

ISBN 1-58660-126-1

Ben-Hur retold by Dan Larsen. © 1990 by Barbour Publishing, Inc.
The Pilgrim's Progress retold by Dan Larsen. © 1989 by Barbour Publishing, Inc.
Robinson Crusoe retold by Dan Larsen. © 1990 by Barbour Publishing, Inc.
The Swiss Family Robinson retold by Kristi Lorene. © 1994 by Barbour Publishing, Inc.

Published by Barbour Publishing, Inc., P.O. Box 719, Uhrichsville, Ohio 44683
http://www.barbourbooks.com

Member of the
Evangelical Christian
Publishers Association

Printed in the United States of America.

CONTENTS

BEN-HUR

A TALE OF THE CHRIST

by Lew Wallace
retold by Dan Larsen

CHAPTER 1

Out of the Jebel es Zubleh mountains and into the desert of Arabia came a traveler riding a camel. The traveler's face was burned brown by the sun, and the black beard that flowed over his face was streaked with gray. He wore a red kerchief on his head and a long white robe.

It was morning. Rider and camel plodded on toward the misty sun rising in the east. Two hours passed, then two more. There were no plants, no animals, no hills, only the wide sea of white sand and the hot sun now in a deep blue sky.

At midday the camel stopped. The rider dismounted, pulled a heavy pack from the camel's back, and set up a small tent. Inside he spread a carpet and laid out bread, dried fruits, smoked mutton, and a leather bottle of wine. He tied a bag of dried beans under the camel's chin for the camel to eat as he wished. Then the man stood and, shading his eyes, scanned the horizon as if looking for someone or something.

The afternoon passed. The man sat in the tent, occasionally going outside to peer off into the distance again. Finally, he saw a speck on the horizon. He felt joy and eagerness at the sight. The speck grew and grew. At last, another camel with a rider stopped just outside the first man's tent.

"Peace to you, O servant of the true God," said the newcomer.

"And to you, O brother of the true faith," replied the first.

They embraced. The first traveler was short and broad, the second tall and gaunt. The first wore the robe and head-dress of an Egyptian, the second the wide pants and short robe of a Hindu.

The Hindu's eyes now shone with tears. "God alone is great!" he said.

"And blessed are they that serve Him!" said the Egyptian. "But now see, the other comes!" He pointed to the north, where a third camel could now be seen coming toward them.

When the third man arrived, he dismounted and bowed to the two. "Peace to you, my brothers," he said. Unlike the Hindu and the Egyptian, this man's face was fair, his hair light and curly. He was bareheaded and wore a short tunic, his legs and arms bare, in the fashion of the Greeks.

"The Spirit brought me here first," said the Egyptian. "Thus I know I am chosen to be servant to my brothers." He washed the others' hands and feet in a bowl of water and dried them with a cloth. "Now come inside," he said. "I have food and drink."

After they had eaten, the Egyptian said, "Before us lie many days together. It is time we knew one another. So if it be agreed, let the one who came last be the first to speak."

So the Greek began. "My tale is a strange one," he said. "I do not understand any of this yet. All I know is that I am doing my master's will. I know it is God's will because I am filled with joy in serving Him.

"I am Gaspar of Athenia, in the land of Greece. My people have long thought that the mind is the best part of man. We are lovers of study and thinking. Our two greatest thinkers taught that every man has a soul and that there is only one God, Who is always just. In my studies, I strove to bring these ideas together, to find the relationship of God to a man's soul. There was no answer in our great schools. So one day, I went to Mount Olympus in northern Thessaly. There I found a cave, where I stayed many days. I believed in God, and I believed He alone could give me the answer I sought, so I prayed day and night.

"My cave overlooked the sea. One day I saw a man flung overboard from a ship. He swam to my shore, and I called to him. I took care of him in my cave. He was a Jew. I learned from him that God does indeed exist and He had been the Jews' lawmaker, ruler, and king for ages. This Jew also said many of his people were expecting God to send a savior to them in Jerusalem, their holy city. People are looking for this savior even now, he said. 'Is this savior only for the Jews?' I asked. 'No,' he said. 'God has kept the Jews as His people so that through them the truth would be kept alive and the rest of the world might be saved.'

"When the Jew had gone, I thought much of these things. One night, I sat in the doorway of my cave, looking at the sky. As I looked, I saw a star appear. It burned brighter and brighter and moved across the sky until it was right overhead. Then I heard a voice: 'Gaspar. Blessed are you! With two others from across the earth, you will see Him Who is promised, and you will be witnesses for Him. In the morning rise, and the Spirit will guide you to meet these other two.' And with the Spirit guiding me, I traveled by ship and then by camel to this very spot here."

The Hindu and the Egyptian wept as they heard this story. Then the Hindu said, "I, too, have a strange tale to tell. My name is Melchior. I am a Hindu by birth. Our people believe in a supreme God, whom we call Brahm. Our sacred poems tell us of virtue, of good works, and of the soul. Our religion teaches that Brahm made four classes in all creation. First are the spirits of heaven and earth. Then the Brahmans, those people most like God Himself. Then the warriors, shepherds, farmers, and merchants. And last, the slaves and servants. My people believe that whoever is born in one of these classes cannot go higher or lower but must remain as he is.

I was born a Brahman. All my life, everything I did was directed by others. I was led, by sacred rituals and ceremonies and study, to follow the life of a Brahman. But I believed that God must be something more than that. I prayed to Him constantly. One day, I discovered the truth that God is love. Thrilled with this, I preached it to everyone, but no one would listen. Some even tried to kill me, so strange was my idea that Brahm is love. The misery of my people made my love grow even more. So finally, I went far up into the mountains, the Himalayas, where I could be alone with God. There I fasted and prayed for my people, asking God to show His love to them as He had to me. One night, I saw a star, just as our friend the Greek did. I heard a voice saying the same things to me, and I have come here, led by the same Spirit."

"Your words, my brother," said the Egyptian, "are spoken in the Spirit of God, and it is in His Spirit that we understand them.

"My name is Balthasar," he continued. "My people of Egypt believed in one God, too—at first. But as the ages passed, we separated the one God into many, and then many more, and yet many more. In this foolishness, we lost our simple faith in a perfect God. But many years ago, a people lived as slaves among my people. These were the Hebrews, who had their own religion and their own God. They were persecuted terribly. But one day, their God delivered them in a way that my people have never forgotten. By this, their God was proved to be the true God. To this day, some of my people believe in the Hebrews' God. I am one of these.

"I, too, saw the star and heard the voice and am come that we might see the savior and worship Him. The voice said to me that we must go to the city of Jerusalem and ask where the king of the Jews is to be born."

The three sat silently for some time, each lost in amazement. Then they rose, held hands, and prayed silently together. Without speaking, they packed up their things, climbed onto their camels, and set out.

The sun was sinking. The night was still, the air cool. The camels went in single file toward the west.

The sun dropped. The night grew cold. The moon rose. The camels went steadily on, casting long moon shadows across the sand.

Suddenly a dazzling light flared up ahead of the travelers,

hanging in the sky just above the horizon. The men shouted together, "The star! The star! God is with us!"

In Jerusalem the people stared at the three travelers of the desert. The camels were unlike any the people had ever seen, so tall and majestic, and the riders were more wondrous still. The rich, embroidered trappings on the saddles and the large, colorful bundles strapped to the camels showed the riders to be rich men from distant lands—perhaps kings.

The three men asked everyone they met, "Where is he that is born king of the Jews?" But no one could answer. Some said, "Go to King Herod and ask him."

So they rode on, coming to the king's palace. When they asked Herod, the king's mouth dropped, and his face grew ashen. *Another king!* he thought. Shaken, he called his priests, who knew what the prophets had written. They met and discussed the question for many hours. Later that night they went to the king. "It is written," said the chief priest, "that the Messiah is to be born in the city of David, Bethlehem of Judea."

Herod told this to the three travelers. Then he said, "Go and find this child and then come and tell me where He is, so I can come and worship Him, too."

The three then rode to Bethlehem, arriving on a clear night. As they entered the city, the star appeared again and traveled through the sky until it stopped directly over a small house on the outskirts of the city.

Here the three men found the child. His mother's name was Mary; her husband was Joseph, a carpenter from Nazareth. The three men knelt and worshipped the child. "How good is God!" said Balthasar, the Egyptian. "He has let us see His savior." Then they gave the baby their gifts of gold, frankincense, and myrrh.

"This child is God's chosen one," said Melchior, the Hindu. "He is sent to save men from their sins."

But that night an angel warned them not to return to Herod, so they returned to their homes by another way.

CHAPTER 2

Twenty-one years after the birth of Christ, Valerius Gratus became the fourth imperial governor of Judea. He was unpopular with the Jews because he tightened Rome's grip on the whole province. His reign marked the beginning of the end of a long, bitter quarrel between the Romans and the Jews.

One day during this time, in a garden of the palace on Mt. Zion, two boys sat talking. One was about nineteen, the other seventeen. Both were black haired and dark skinned. The elder, Messala, was a Roman; the younger, Judah, a Jew. The boys had been childhood friends. Messala's father was a Roman tax collector in Jerusalem. Messala had been sent to Rome to be educated, where he had stayed for five years. Now he was home again. He had gone a happy child and come back a Roman—vain, almost scornful, his lip curled slightly in a proud sneer as he spoke to his younger friend.

"A Jew never changes, does he?" said Messala, laughing. "Your lives go nowhere, just round and round. What is there in your religion but doddering old men arguing over worthless things? You have no poetry, no art. Your masters, your teachers—what are they, compared with our masters in Rome, who teach everything that is worth knowing?"

The Jew's face was flushed. He had grown more and more sullen as the other spoke. Now he rose to leave.

"No, no, keep your place!" cried Messala.

"You mock me," said Judah.

"Hear me further," said Messala. "In my teacher's last lecture in Rome he said, 'Mars reigns, and Eros is dead.' He meant war is everything, love nothing. So it is with Rome. There is much yet in the world for us to conquer. See what possibilities lie before a Roman! I am a soldier. Why not you, too? I am a soldier now, but one day I will be a prefect. Think of life in Rome with money, wine, women, games, poets at the banquets, intrigues in the court, dice all the year-round! You can share this with me. Judea is rich and ripe for plunder. When I have grown fat from her, I will make you high priest." He burst into laughter.

"We had better part," said Judah sadly. "I wish I had not come. I sought a friend and find a—"

"A Roman," said Messala, laughing again. "Be wise. Give up the follies of Moses and the traditions. They are dead things. Rome is the world now."

Judah walked to the gate of the garden. "You have made me suffer today," he said. "You have convinced me that we can never be the friends we were, not ever." He left the garden.

Messala stood silently for a moment as if thinking. Then he shrugged. "So be it," he said. "Eros is dead. Mars reigns."

Just off the Via Dolorosa, a main street in Jerusalem, sat the Hur house, enclosed by a thick stone wall. The house had two stories and was very well built and richly furnished. Judah's father had been a very rich merchant but had been lost at sea many years earlier. The boy now lived here with his mother, younger sister, and their servants. Judah's favorite servant was Amrah, an old Egyptian woman who had served the family for many years and was loved as one of the family.

That afternoon, when the boy came home, he flung himself onto a couch in the courtyard and lay with his face buried in his arms until evening.

Amrah came into the courtyard. "Supper is over, and it is late," she said. "Is my son not hungry?"

"No," he said.

"Are you sick?"

"No, not sick. Life does not seem so pleasant as it did this morning." But he would say nothing more.

Amrah loved the boy as her own son. "Your mother is on the roof," she said. "Go and talk to her."

The roof was like another room of the house. A low wall made of tiles ran around the edge. There were chairs and couches for people to rest on and a little pavilion with open sides in the center. Many houses in the region were like this. During the day, people sought shelter from the desert heat, but at night the air was cool, the sky clear and beautiful. Roofs were used for eating and gathering of families and friends and for sleeping.

Judah's mother was on the roof tonight. She lay on a couch in the pavilion, watching the stars. At her son's approach, she sat up. She could tell he was troubled.

"I visited Messala today," Judah said. "He is very much changed. He mocks our religion, our customs. He could have at least remembered our friendship. But he is no longer a friend. He is a—a Roman."

His mother was silent for awhile, lost in thought. Finally she said, "There has never been a great nation that did not think itself superior to all others. When the Roman laughs at Israel, he repeats the folly of other nations who have conquered us before. Egypt, Assyria, Macedonia—all have held Jerusalem, as Rome does now. But they have all gone, my son, and Jerusalem still stands, unchanged. He who laughs at Israel laughs at God."

Judah's eyes brightened a little.

"There is no comparison possible between Israel and Rome," his mother continued. "While Israel has at times forgotten God, Rome never knew Him. We are God's people. He will answer any charges brought against us."

The boy's heart was beating fast. "And I?" he said. "What am I to be, Mother?"

"Just serve the Lord, the Lord God of Israel, not Rome," she said.

"May I be a soldier, then?"

"Yes. Did not Moses call God a man of war? But if you will be a soldier, serve the Lord, not Caesar." She rose then and, kissing her son good night, went inside.

Judah fell asleep on the roof. His heart no longer troubled him. When he woke, it was to the sound of music and singing. The sun was up, and his sister, Tirzah, sat near him. She was fifteen, as beautiful as her brother was handsome. She played a stringed instrument as she sang. Judah lay there smiling until she finished the song.

"Very pretty, my Tirzah, very pretty," he said.

She smiled. "The song?" she asked.

"Yes, and the singer, too. It sounds Greek. Where did you get it?"

"I heard it at the theater last month."

"Have you any more like it?"

"Yes, but not now. Amrah is bringing our breakfast to us up here. She says you are not well."

"I'm fine," he said. And he told her of his visit with Messala the day before.

"What do you think, Tirzah?" he asked. "I am going away."

"Going away!" she said, "Where? When? For what?"

He laughed. "Three questions, all in one breath! I am going to Rome to be a soldier."

Her smile faded. "You will be killed!"

"If God wills, then yes. But, Tirzah, not all soldiers are killed."

She began to weep. "But we are so happy here. Stay with us. Why should you go off to Rome?"

"War is a trade. To learn it well, one must go to school, and there is no school like a Roman camp."

"But you would not fight for Rome?" she asked.

"Yes," he said, "if in return I learn how to fight against Rome one day. Now, be still! I hear Amrah coming. Say nothing of this to her."

The two had just started eating when suddenly the sounds of trumpets rose from the street below. Brother and sister rushed to the wall to look.

Down the street came a procession of Roman soldiers. In

the middle of the column of soldiers rode an official on horseback. He wore no armor and carried no weapon. His robe was embroidered with yellow silk. His appearance seemed to excite the anger of people along the street, who now could be seen leaning over the walls of roofs like the one of the Hur house. "Robber!" they shouted. "Dog of a Roman! Gratus the dog!"

Gratus! thought Judah. *So this is he. No wonder the people are so angry.* All Jerusalem hated the Roman tyrant. But Judah's thoughts were not really on Gratus. He was watching the soldiers. Look at the brawny limbs of those men! The sharp spears! The shiny helmets and breastplates! In his excitement, he leaned farther over the wall.

Crack! A piece of tile broke loose under his weight. It began to fall, and the governor was directly below! Judah reached for the tile, shouting. Below on the street, faces turned up to him, in time to see what looked like a boy throwing a heavy piece of tile down.

And as if the hand of fate were stretched against the family of Hur, the tile struck the governor on the head, and he fell from his horse as though dead.

Judah stumbled back from the wall, his face white. "Tirzah!" he cried. "I have killed the governor!"

Now all along the street rose a cheer. The people saw the tile fall, saw the governor struck, and, like the soldiers, they thought the boy had thrown it. Now, goaded by the fall of their hated governor, the people swarmed into the street, attacking the soldiers with clubs, kitchen knives—anything they could grab. The battle surged all through the street, but it was a slaughter. The soldiers quickly cut their way through the mob.

The sound of cracking timbers and crunching stone came from below.

"They are taking our house!" Judah shouted. Up came the screams and shouts of servants, the clang of swords and spears, and the tramp of soldiers' feet.

"Mother! Mother!" screamed Judah as he leapt down the stairs. Soldiers poured into the courtyard through the broken-in gate.

"That is he!" came a sharp voice. Judah turned. Messala! He was pointing at Judah, his face twisted with hate.

"Him?" said a tall man in legionary armor. "He is but a boy!"

"He is the one!" Messala snapped. "And there, his mother and sister. You have them all."

"Messala!" cried Judah. "My mother and sister! Help them! Remember our childhood, I pray you!"

Messala did not even look at Judah. He just turned on his heels and walked into the street.

Judah's heart turned to ice. Messala! "In the hour of Your vengeance, Lord, let mine be the hand to deliver it to him!" he prayed.

In the street, the governor was being led off, his head wrapped. *So he is not dead!* thought Judah. *They will listen to me. They will understand it was an accident.*

But his hands were tied behind his back. A trumpet sounded, and the soldiers moved off down the street, pushing and dragging Judah along with them. He could not look back, could not see what had happened to his mother and sister. He pleaded with the tall soldier to let him explain to the governor.

The soldier's face was grim. "The governor has already determined your fate," he said.

"Now move on and be silent!"

CHAPTER 3

On the western coast of Italy, the city of Misenum sat atop a hill overlooking the bay of Neapolis. It was hard to tell which was bluer that day, the clear sky or the sparkling water of the bay. The waves rolled in softly to the white, sandy shore.

At anchor in the bay was half the reserve navy of Rome, about a hundred warships. Their sails were furled, and in each ship a hundred and twenty long oars rested in the water, sixty to a side.

A stone wall surrounded the city on the hill. A narrow road passed through an opening in this wall and meandered down the hill to the bay. Along this road now came about thirty men, officials by their looks. They wore long white togas bordered with purple. The man leading was about fifty, slightly bald, and wearing a crown of laurel leaves.

When they reached the shore, the other men began to say their farewells to the one wearing the laurel crown.

"Where will you seek these pirates, my good Quintus Arrius?" asked one of the men.

"They were seen in the Aegean Sea, according to the letter I received from Sejanus," said Arrius, a Roman tribune. "If you have any offerings, my friends, pray to the gods for good sailing and strong rowing. But look, there is my ship."

The ship was a fighter, long, narrow, and low. Just under the waterline on the front of the ship was a long, wooden beak, its tip shod with steel. This was used to ram enemy ships at sea. A trumpet sounded on board, and out of the hatchways came the fighting men, lining up on deck. As one, they saluted the tribune. Sunlight gleamed off their polished helmets and shields.

"Now I am away to my duty, my friends," said the tribune.

"The gods go with you, O Quintus," said one of the men. They each came up to embrace the tribune.

"Farewell," he said. As he walked up the ramp to the ship, trumpets blared out from all the ships in the bay.

By noon, the fleet was skimming the sea along the southwestern Italian coast. To a sailor or a merchant on shore, the sight of a hundred Roman warships could mean only one thing: Rome was looking for pirates. A group of about thirty Greek pirate ships had been ravaging the coasts in this area for many months. The reports of these pirates, who plundered and sank ships, had reached Caesar, and now he was acting.

The tribune, Quintus Arrius, was an important military official in Rome. As commander of this fleet, he was under orders to attack and destroy the entire pirate fleet. He spoke to the chief of the rowers, a man called the hortator.

"My orders say we are to go past the Camponellan Cape to Messina," said Arrius. "Beyond that, follow the bend of the Calabrian shore till Melito is on our left, then head eastward for Cythera. The gods willing, we will not anchor until we are in the Bay of Antemona. Out duty is urgent. We will need all speed. I am relying on you."

The hortator bowed and returned to his post. In the middle

of the ship was a cabin with the rowers' benches. In its front was a raised platform where the chief of the rowers sat beating on a basin to mark the tempo of the oars. Farther toward the front and above this platform was another platform, where the tribune sat. The rowers were slaves, all of them prisoners condemned to the galleys for life. They sat at their places and rowed, eating and sleeping during their brief rest periods. This was their whole life. A man condemned to the galleys usually lived no more than a year under such extreme circumstances. There were men of many sorts—blacks, Jews, Egyptians, Gauls, red-haired, pale-skinned savages from Hibernia, black-haired, blue-eyed giants of the Cimbri—each chosen for his brawn and endurance. Their names were forgotten; they were only known by the numbers painted at their places on the benches.

Arrius liked to watch the rowers. He was a lover of strength and physical sports. As he watched the men, he noted their various strengths or weaknesses, deciding who might need to be replaced by a fresh rower. He took particular interest in one rower—number sixty. This one was no more than a boy. *Yet what a boy!* thought Arrius. His black hair was shaggy as a lion's mane and hung down to his shoulders. His beard was still scanty and barely covered his cheeks. His neck was thick, his shoulders rounded. Thick biceps rolled like melons under the strain of pulling on the oar. The sinews in his forearms stood out like steel cables. Under his grasp, his heavy oak oar almost bent to breaking.

By the gods, what strength! thought Arrius. *He has spirit!*

I must know more of him.

Two days later, Arrius told the chief to send number sixty to him on the deck.

The youth walked slowly up to Arrius, his face showing curiosity. In three years at the oars, he had not once stepped outside the cabin.

"The hortator tells me you are his best rower," Arrius said.

"The hortator is very kind," said the youth.

"You have been here three years," said Arrius. "How is it that you have survived so long? Most men can last only a year here."

"The noble Arrius forgets that a man's spirit has much to do with his endurance. By its help, the weak sometimes thrive while the strong perish."

"By your speech, you are a Jew. I have not been to Jerusalem, but I knew one of its princes. He was fit to have been a king. What is your family name?"

"My father was a prince of Jerusalem who was known and honored by the great Augustus of Rome. His name was Ithanar, of the house of Hur. I am Judah. By my father's family, I would now be called Ben-Hur."

The tribune stepped back. "A son of Hur!" he said. "What has brought you here?"

"I was accused of trying to murder Valerius Gratus, the governor."

"You! You are that one?" The tribune's mouth was wide open. "I heard that story. I thought that family had been blotted off the earth."

There was pain in Ben-Hur's voice. "O noble tribune," he said, almost weeping, "my mother! And my little Tirzah! Can you tell me if they live? And if so, are they well?" His lips quivered. "That horrible day is three years gone now, but every hour has been an eternity to me. A lifetime in a bottomless pit with death, and no relief but in labor. And in all that time not a word from anyone, not a whisper. Oh, if in being forgotten we could only forget! If only I could hide from that scene—my sister torn from me, my mother's last look! I have felt the shock of ships in battle, felt the tempest lashing the sea, and laughed when others prayed. Death would be relief to me. In the strain of bending the oar, I have sought to escape the pain of that day. I can never be happy while they are lost. They call me every night in my dreams." The tears poured down his cheeks. And now his voice turned bitter. "And mine was the hand that brought them down!"

"Do you admit your guilt then?" asked Arrius.

The youth's eyes flashed. He drew his shoulders back. "I swear by the God of my people, our God from the very beginning, that I am innocent!" he said.

The tribune's face grew troubled. "Did you not have a trial?" he asked.

"No."

"No trial!" cried the tribune. "No witnesses? Who judged you?"

"They bound me with cords," said Ben-Hur. "I saw no one. No one spoke to me. They dragged me to the seaside. I have been a galley slave since."

Arrius was deeply troubled. The Romans were lovers of justice! It was impossible to condemn a man without a fair trial under Roman law. What had happened here? Arrius wondered. What horrible scheme—and whose—had it been to destroy this family? He believed Ben-Hur's story. The youth's feelings showed too strongly for it to be a lie. Arrius decided that he would check into it when he returned to Rome. For now, he sent Ben-Hur back to his bench.

That night at his oar, Ben-Hur looked at the starry sky through his air vent. "Oh, Lord," he prayed, "I am a true son of the Israel You have loved. Help me, I pray You!"

And all through the Roman fleet, the message was stirring: The enemy has been sighted. Prepare for battle!

They came on the pirate fleet in the dark of night. The steel-shod prows of the Roman galleys battered the Greek vessels into splinters. Many sank almost immediately, but many more roused themselves for battle. From out of the darkness came battle cries, the clashing of spears as they cascaded onto the decks, and the splintering of wooden ships being smashed to pieces. And now fires flared up all over the ocean's surface as the Romans hurled burning oily rags onto the enemy ships. Soon several ships were engulfed in roaring flames. Men dove screaming into the churning water.

The rowers could only hear the sounds of battle. They had been in many such battles, and their rowing did not change a beat. If their masters won this battle, nothing changed for the slaves. If the enemy won, the slaves might be taken by new masters, but their life of rowing would go on just the same. It made no difference to them.

During battles at sea, the Romans chained the rowers' ankles so they could not escape. If a Roman ship was sunk, the slaves went down with it, chained to their benches. This was the one horror for a galley slave in battle, so they rowed fiercely, keeping their ship out of reach of enemy battering rams.

But that night, Arrius had told the chief to leave Ben-Hur's ankles free. *Why?* thought Ben-Hur. His heart was pounding. From up on deck came the clamor of shouting men and clanging swords and spears. The ship had been boarded by pirates! Ben-Hur dropped his oar. He sat still, the blood pounding in his temples. Suddenly he decided. He jumped from his bench, cleared the few stairs to the deck in one leap, and burst out of the cabin.

Just then the deck lurched. From below came a deafening crunch. Pirates had rammed the ship! Ben-Hur was thrown on his face. As he struggled to his feet, the sea rushed in through the wrecked side. A wall of water smashed into him and carried him overboard like a dry leaf in a tempest.

Ben-Hur struggled underwater until his lungs were ready to burst. When his head shot up to the surface, the ship was gone. He swam to a floating timber and dragged himself onto it, clinging there, gasping for breath. Suddenly a Roman helmet emerged from the sea by his side, then a hand. Ben-Hur grabbed the wrist and heaved a man onto the timber. Arrius! His face was ghostly pale, his eyes wide and staring, but he was still alive. His breath came in shallow gasps, his lips trembling.

Through the night, Ben-Hur lay on the timber as the battle continued. The timber drifted farther and farther away. When morning came, Arrius woke. He stared around him at the calm sea and at Ben-Hur.

Then he struggled to sit up, reaching a hand to Ben-Hur. "Son of Hur," he said, "I knew your father and loved him. You have saved me. If we are rescued, I swear to you that I will take you to Rome. You will be my son and heir. Everything I have will be yours!"

CHAPTER 4

Up the river Orantes to the docks of Antioch in Assyria came a transport galley. It docked and began to unload cargo on the busy wharf as several passengers stepped ashore. One of these walked up the narrow street into the city. His white robe flowed over him loosely, yet it was stretched taut over his broad shoulders. The hands and forearms that hung from his short sleeves showed an immense strength. Three years as a galley rower and five more in the best military schools of Rome had developed Ben-Hur to the peak of his physical powers. Five years as the adopted son of Roman tribune Quintus Arrius had also developed a noble manner. His movements were smooth and graceful, barely concealing his explosive strength.

Arrius, the tribune, had died at sea three years ago, leaving Ben-Hur sole heir to his vast estate in the city of Misenum. The young Hur, now calling himself Arrius, had been trained in the military schools, learning all the arts of weapons and fighting. He had been an eager pupil, his hatred for Rome and his desire for revenge driving him on. He attacked his training with a ferocity that eventually earned him a reputation throughout Rome. For his swordsmanship and his wrestling skills, he had become famous in the palestra, the training school of the gladiators.

At Arrius's death, Ben-Hur took over his father's duties.

He was in Antioch now on official business. But just now he had another purpose. He walked quickly through the winding street that bustled with merchants and peddlers with laden carts. He turned onto a street that led past the wharves by the shore. It went through an old stone gateway and under the Selucian bridge, a great arched walkway overhead. Here Ben-Hur stopped. Under the bridge was a gray stone house with a heavy wooden door. He knocked and a porter answered.

"I wish to see Simonides the merchant," said Ben-Hur.

"This way, Sir," said the porter. He led Ben-Hur by a path through stacks and stacks of boxes and bags of cargo, up a stairway, to a small stone building on the roof. "There," said the porter.

Ben-Hur called at the door.

"In God's name, come in," said a little man. He was sitting, or seemed to be propped up, in a heap of cushions on the floor. His head rested on his chest as if he had no neck. His body was a shapeless lump under a loose silk robe. By his side stood a girl, black haired and beautiful. She looked at Ben-Hur shyly.

"Are you Simonides, merchant and Jew?" asked Ben-Hur.

"I am he," said the man. "And this is my daughter, Esther. Please state your business, Sir."

"I am the son of Ithanar, late head of the house of Hur in Jerusalem," said Ben-Hur. The merchant's right hand closed tightly into a fist for an instant. "I heard a tale on my voyage to Antioch," continued Ben-Hur. "A certain man on board told of a man named Simonides who has become very wealthy by trading. This man said that Simonides had been the chief servant of my father in Jerusalem and managed my father's business from Antioch."

The merchant's face seemed pale, and his hand again closed tightly, but he said nothing.

"I also heard that this Simonides was sought by the governor Gratus and tortured until he confessed that his wealth was illegal," said Ben-Hur.

"You have heard rightly in one thing," said Simonides. "I was indeed tortured twice. My body was broken. It is now useless to me. But Gratus could not break my spirit. My wealth is from trading and is legally mine. As to the other, yes, I knew your father, but that is all I will say. First, I must see some proof that you are who you say you are."

Proof! Ben-Hur had not thought of that. "I can prove my Roman identity," he said, "but not my other." He told Simonides his story, from the accident to Gratus to the present. "But do not think that I have come to demand my father's property," continued Ben-Hur. "You may keep all of it. All I wish to know is whether my mother and sister still live, and where. Can you tell me?"

"I heard of the tragedy to your family," said Simonides. "And I did seek to know whether your mother and sister were alive. But no one has heard of them since that day. I believe they are lost."

Ben-Hur struggled against tears. "Then I, too, am lost!" he said. He turned to leave. "I pray your pardon for my intrusion."

His voice shook slightly. "I would not have troubled you at all but for my sorrow. Now I have nothing to live for but vengeance. Farewell."

"Peace go with you," said Simonides.

Esther could not speak. She was sobbing, her face in her hands.

As soon as Ben-Hur was gone, Simonides turned to his daughter. A smile lit his pallid face. "Esther, quick!" he said. "Bring Malluch to me."

Ben-Hur wandered about the city aimlessly. On hearing about Simonides, a hope had sprung up in his heart, but now it was crushed again. One thought would sustain him: Vengeance! Rome would pay!

Now as he walked, great crowds of people began pushing past him. They were moving quickly. He went with them to see where they were going. Soon a man appeared at his side wearing a simple robe and carrying a wooden staff. On his head was a brown cloth tied with yellow rope.

"Sir," said Ben-Hur, "are you a Hebrew? You have the look of one."

"That I am," said the man, smiling. "I am from Jerusalem. Are you going my way?"

"I will, gladly. Where are all these people going?"

"To the stadium. The chariots are practicing today. Come."

The two men talked as they went. To the stranger's questions Ben-Hur would only tell him that he was a Jew but an official of Rome, in Antioch on official business. But

Ben-Hur began to like this man. It had been so long since he had seen a countryman. He asked the stranger for any news he had from Jerusalem.

The stadium was filling with people. Ben-Hur and the Jew took seats near the arena. The chariots were circling the track slowly, parading all their finery. One particular chariot caught Ben-Hur's eye. It was Roman in style and lavished with gold trappings. As it came around the bend, he could see the driver's face.

Messala!

Ben-Hur's heart jumped. There was that slight sneer, that proud tilt of the head. How long had he waited for a chance to meet him again? And how long had he nursed thoughts of revenge? Now here he was!

Just then his attention was drawn by a man's shouting voice. In front near the track stood a bearded man in a turban, waving his arms to the spectators. "Men of the East and West, hearken!" he cried. "I bring you word from Sheik Ilderim. With four horses, he comes up against the best here. He needs a mighty man to drive them. To whoever can handle them in the chariot race he promises riches forever! I say to you all, tell everyone of this offer."

"Who is this man he speaks of?" Ben-Hur asked his companion.

"Sheik Ilderim is a mighty man of the desert," said the Jew. "He has many people, many horses, many camels. Some say he controls all the goings to and fro in the desert."

Ben-Hur could barely control his excitement. "My friend,"

he said, "tell me. Can a man forget his mother?"

"If he's an Israelite, never!" said the other. "Our commandment is, 'Honor your mother and father as long as you live.' "

"By your words I know you are a true Jew," Ben-Hur said. "And I know I can trust you. Listen. I know that man there." He pointed to Messala. Then he told the Jew as much of his story as he dared, leaving out his real name and his life as a slave on the galley.

"Tell me," continued Ben-Hur. "Do you know where to find this Sheik Ilderim? I wish to be his driver."

"Do you know how to drive?" asked the Jew.

"I was trained by the best in Rome. I have driven chariots for the emperor himself."

"The sheik is camped in the Orchard of Palms. I can take you to him."

"Can we go tonight?"

"We can start right now."

"You are a true friend! But tell me, what is your name?"

"I am Malluch," said the man, bowing.

It was two hours by horse to the Orchard of Palms, but Ben-Hur and Malluch talked as they rode.

"For his treachery and his taking my mother and sister from me, I wish to punish this man Messala," said Ben-Hur. "Will you help me?"

"I am a Jew, not a Roman," said Malluch. "As you are a Jew, we are brothers. Yes, I will help you. I am no friend of Rome. And it is the law of Moses: An eye for an eye and a tooth for a tooth."

"Is this chariot race an important event here?"

"In Antioch, there is none more important. Thousands upon thousands of people from all over the world will be here."

For the first time in many years, Ben-Hur smiled.

CHAPTER 5

The four horses were Arabians—beautiful, graceful, strong. Under Ben-Hur's hand they drove as one horse, flowing swiftly across the sand. Sheik Ilderim and Malluch stood watching as Ben-Hur practiced. The sheik's eyes were dancing.

"It takes a gifted hand to make those horses run like that," he said. "But, see? They are yet just loping. When they are given rein, none can match them!"

Ben-Hur and Malluch had arrived last night. The sheik greeted Malluch as an old friend. Ben-Hur wondered about this. Then he offered to drive the sheik's horses. He suggested that he would try them today. Ilderim could watch him with them before deciding on him as a driver. The sheik agreed. He then served them richly. They ate and drank sitting on thick cushions in the sheik's tent.

For hours the next day, Ben-Hur drove the horses. Then he ate with the sheik again that night.

"I have a guest with me," said the sheik. "He is dining with us tonight. He has a story to tell that an Israelite should never tire of hearing. Ah, here he is. Come in, Balthasar, my friend."

An old man entered the tent. His beard was even longer and whiter than the old sheik's. He wore a black robe.

"To you and your friend I give peace and the blessing of

the one true God," he said.

As they ate, Balthasar the Egyptian told Ben-Hur the story of the meeting of the wise men and the birth of the Messiah. As Ben-Hur listened, the beating of his heart quickened.

"And when we had seen the child in Bethlehem," continued Balthasar, "we were warned in a vision not to tell Herod the king, because he would try to kill the child. And the husband of the child's mother was warned to take the child and flee into Egypt."

Ben-Hur believed every word of this. He was a Jew and was taught the laws and promises of the Holy Scriptures. He well knew the promise of the coming king of the Jews. "So," he said, "this king must be alive now."

"He would be about your age," said Balthasar.

"And this king is to rule all of Israel?"

"His kingdom will last forever."

A new thought struck Ben-Hur. A king! A king to rule all Israel, to destroy Roman power forever! He stayed awake long into the night thinking, too excited to sleep.

The next morning a messenger rode up to the camp. "The merchant Simonides wishes to see you," he said to Ben-Hur.

When he stepped inside the roof office of Simonides later that day, Ben-Hur stopped short and blinked in surprise. There sat the merchant and his daughter as before, but with him now were the sheik, Balthasar, and the Jew named Malluch.

"What does this mean?" asked Ben-Hur. There was danger in his voice.

"Please sit down," said Simonides, pointing to a chair.

As Ben-Hur listened in amazement, the merchant told him he had sent his servant, Malluch, to watch him, to see whether he was really who he claimed to be. Malluch reported that Ben-Hur did indeed seem to be telling the truth.

Simonides pointed to the sheik and Balthasar.

"These, too, are my friends," he said. "They, too, have talked with you, and they speak well of you. I am indeed your father's servant. During his life I operated here in Antioch. When that Roman dog Gratus took your mother and sister and your home, he had me brought to him to get from me the rest of your father's wealth. I refused him, so he had me tortured, twice. The second time, when they brought me home broken as you see me now, my beloved wife, Rachel, fell dead of grief at seeing me." His eyes filled with tears. His daughter clutched his shoulder.

"But Gratus could not take from me what I was entrusted by your father to keep," continued Simonides. "Now I return to you all I have earned. The total of your wealth, son of Hur, is six hundred and seventy-three talents, making you the richest subject in the world."

Ben-Hur stammered, "Dear Simonides, my father's faithful servant! How could a man be better served? I wish to free you from your servitude. All that you have, all you have earned, I give you and your daughter. It is all yours to keep."

"No, good master," said Simonides. "I chose to be your father's bond servant for life because I loved him. I do not wish the service to end with his son. Let me remain as your servant. Only entrust the managing of your property to me, as your father did. This is all I ask of you."

"As you wish," said Ben-Hur, bowing.

"There is one thing more I would ask of you," said Simonides.

"Balthasar has told you of the coming king. This king is no doubt somewhere preparing for the moment He declares himself. When He comes, He will need the power to crush Rome. With your wealth and your mastery of the arts of war, you could be of more service to Him than anyone on earth."

Ben-Hur's hands gripped the arms of his chair. His heart was pounding.

"Think of my grievance with Rome!" continued Simonides. "Is it not at least equal to yours? With our wealth we could arm thousands of faithful Israelites to fight for the king. And you yourself could train them and lead them in battle. The good sheik will help you. He will show you the most desolate places in the desert, where the troops can train. His people control the desert. They will guard you."

"And when the king makes His appearance, His army will be ready and waiting!" cried Ben-Hur.

Simonides nodded. "And what better revenge against Rome could you and I wish for?" he said.

The old Egyptian shook his head sadly. "Ah, you do not understand," he said. "The king will not come with swords. The kingdom He rules does not belong to this earth. He has come to save men's souls, not to save Israel from Rome."

Ben-Hur seemed not to hear. "I will begin as soon as possible," he said, rising. "I will work from the desert, and you, my good Simonides, from your seat in Antioch here. But first I have a score to settle with an old enemy. The chariot race is in five days. I must get the horses ready!"

Back at the sheik's camp, Ben-Hur drove the horses for several hours daily. He was an expert in chariot racing, and he knew these were the best horses he had ever driven. All through Antioch, excitement was mounting over the day of the race. Huge bets had been placed, most of them on Messala, and Messala had bet his entire fortune on himself. This was even better than Ben-Hur had hoped for. If Messala lost, he would not only be shamed in all of Rome, but he would be brought to poverty, as well. The taste of revenge grew sweeter in Ben-Hur's mouth with each passing hour.

One afternoon Sheik Ilderim came to Ben-Hur. He was holding a letter. His face was grave. "My people guard all the roads through the desert," he said. "Early this morning one of my men stopped a courier on his way to Jerusalem. This courier carried a letter from Messala to Governor Gratus."

Ben-Hur's face suddenly paled.

"Messala told the governor that the man they had sent away to be a galley slave was now here in Antioch. He also said that if this man, Ben-Hur, were not destroyed, then all the wealth he, Messala, and the governor had stolen from the family of Hur might be lost to them."

Ben-Hur could not speak. His heart was racing. He turned, stumbled into his tent, and lay panting on the ground. How? How could Messala have known? Had he recognized him? Had someone told him? And it had been a plot? Messala and

Gratus had used the accident to Gratus as an excuse to put Ben-Hur and his mother and sister away and steal their property.

The sheik entered Ben-Hur's tent. "After the race we must flee," he said. "Gratus will send troops here to destroy us. Messala knows about me. He knows you are staying with me. We are not in danger until after the race, but then we must flee and leave no trace. They cannot pursue us into the desert. The desert is mine. They know that there my people would hunt them down and destroy them like wandering cattle. I will stand by you, Ben-Hur. And I will help you prepare your army in the desert for the coming king."

Ben-Hur stood and embraced the sheik. "Tomorrow," he said. "Tomorrow I will have my revenge against Messala. And his destruction will be our first strike against Rome."

At three o'clock the next afternoon, the stadium was filled with people. They had come from as far away as Rome to see this chariot race. They chanted and waved banners for their favorites.

Just then trumpets sounded. Out came the chariots. The crowd roared. The chariots slowly circled the track, each carrying a flag of a different color: Ben-Hur's was white, Messala's, scarlet. These were the colors waved by most in the crowd. Of the two, there were perhaps more white than scarlet.

Eight chariots circled the dusty track. A hundred thousand spectators shouted and waved and pounded their feet on the stone steps of the vast Olympian stadium. In the front row were the sheik, Balthasar, Simonides, Malluch, and Esther. She alone in all that crowd was silent. She watched Ben-Hur.

The chariots came around the bend once more and drew together in a line across the track. Then a trumpet sounded, and the race was on.

Messala was in front. In the stadium his color waved wildly. Thirty-two horses pounded around the track, whips lashing over their backs, dirt clods flying.

Two laps were down. Messala still led. The sneer on his face seemed to widen with each trip around the track. Ben-Hur's face was calm, but his jaw was set firmly. He seemed strangely reserved, as if waiting for something.

Four laps were down. Ben-Hur had pulled even with Messala. Suddenly Messala lashed out with his whip, striking Ben-Hur across the cheek. Ben-Hur staggered and almost fell. A gasp went up from the crowd. The Romans among the crowd cheered and shouted and chanted Messala's name.

But Ben-Hur recovered, though he had lost ground. Five laps. Six. Messala had stretched his lead. A cold light shone in his eyes. His teeth were set in a hard grin. Now Ben-Hur was only midpack.

Seven laps. "Messala! Messala!" came the chants. Only Ben-Hur's small group of friends sat unmoving, unspeaking. The sheik's face was pale, his lips tight. Esther was weeping.

Eight laps. Nine. The sheik dropped his chin to his chest. He seemed shrunken. His lips quivered.

Ten Laps. "Look!" cried Esther.

Messala was way out in front, but now Ben-Hur's chariot broke from the pack, his whip snaked over the Arabians' backs as they leapt forward. Around the turn came Messala and Ben-Hur, almost together. Suddenly Ben-Hur jerked his reins, bringing his chariot wheel just inside Messala's. His wheel touched the other's axle. *Crack!* Messala's chariot lurched, throwing him over the front. He tumbled along the track under the wheels of the chariot, then lay still in the dust, and Ben-Hur drove across the finish line the victor.

CHAPTER 6

The first thing Simonides did with Ben-Hur's money was to get rid of Valerius Gratus, governor of Judea in Jerusalem. Simonides paid Sejanus, the imperial favorite in Rome, five talents in Roman money to remove Gratus from office. In Gratus's place, Sejanus appointed Pontius Pilate.

Simonides did this for Ben-Hur, who was going to Jerusalem to look for his mother and sister. Without Gratus, Ben-Hur would be freer to search the city.

While Gratus had been cold and hateful, Pilate had some measure of good in his heart. The first thing he did in office was to review the records of all the prisoners Gratus had kept. Many of these prisoners were set free from the vast dungeons under the palace tower.

One particular cell was discovered deep underground. Gratus had erased all records of this cell from the prison documents. It was sealed off from all others. He had told the warden that two men with leprosy, both condemned to life in prison for murder, were kept there. No one but Gratus knew who the occupants of that cell were.

When the cell was opened, there were not two men but two women inside. They were naked and starved almost to death. Their thin white hair hung in tatters. And worse—they were lepers! Their lips and noses had been half eaten by the disease. Their skin was sickly white and covered with scaly patches; their voices were shrill and harsh. Seeing them, the warden drew back in horror.

They were given clothes and set free. That night, the two women hobbled through the dark city streets, holding on to each other for support. They stared about them in wonder, as if seeing the outside world for the first time.

Slowly, painfully, they made their way through the city. Halfway down a street called the Via Dolorosa they stopped at a large house enclosed by a stone wall. The house was dark. Vines and creepers covered the stone wall. The gates had been sealed with mortar and timbers. A plaque on one gate read, "This is the Property of the Emperor."

The women stood for a long time looking at the house and weeping. Suddenly one grabbed the other's arm. "Mother!" she whispered. "There is someone lying under the tree by the gate."

Just then the figure turned, and the moon shone on his face.

"Judah!" gasped one of the women. "It is my Judah!" The other woman started across the street but was grabbed by the first. "No, Tirzah!" she whispered sharply. "Do not touch him! We are lepers. If you touch him, he will get the disease."

They stood there, wringing their hands and weeping bitterly. Then one of them crept across the street to the sleeping man. She knelt at his feet. "Judah, my son, my dear son," she sobbed softly. "I shall never see you again. But it is enough that God has let me see that you live and that you are well." And she kissed the dirty soles of his sandals. Then she went back to the other woman. They continued on down the street, looking back at the man, their weeping growing louder and more agonized as they went. Soon they came to a gate in the city wall, turned, and went out into the desert.

They did not see the silent figure stealing down the street and stopping at the house they had just left. The figure almost stumbled over the sleeping man.

"Judah!" came a woman's voice. The man woke. He stared up at the little woman wrapped in a cloak and shawl.

"Amrah!" he cried. "Is it you?" He climbed to his feet.

"It is," she said. "And praise to the God of your race! I thought you were long dead."

They held each other tightly, sobbing and laughing.

"It is a long time since I heard my boyhood name, Judah," said the man. "I have taken my father's name now—Ben-Hur."

"Come inside," said Amrah. She reached a hand in through the timbers in the gate. There was a click, and the gate swung open.

They went quickly across the dark, silent courtyard. Tall weeds grew in cracks among the flagstones. The walls of the house were darkened with disuse, and here and there were patches of lichen.

Inside, Amrah drew a shutter across a window and lit a small lamp. And there in the dim light stood Amrah as Ben-Hur remembered her. Amrah the beloved, faithful maid-servant. She was a bit older looking, a bit more stooped, but her loving gaze was just the same.

"Amrah," said Ben-Hur, "how is it that you are here? Have you lived here alone all this time?"

She nodded. Her eyes glistened. "Perhaps you did not see," she said, "but that evil day the soldiers came into our home and took—took"—here she broke and began sobbing, her face in her hands—"took your dear little sister Tirzah, your mother, and you, the soldiers grabbed me, too. But I broke away and fled through the confusion back into the house. I was sealed in. I had food enough for awhile, but soon I needed to go into the city. I worked away at the mortar on the gate we entered tonight until I had loosened enough so I could work the latch. From the outside it still appears sealed. I go out to buy food only at night, and I have lived here in secret all these years. I have prayed every day that someday at least one of you would return to me. And now you have come, my Judah."

She held out her arms to him and wept on his shoulder as they held each other.

"You must tell me, Amrah," he said, "though my heart fails me as I ask. Are my—Have you heard of my mother and sister?"

There was pain and bitterness in her voice as she said, "They were taken to the dungeons under the tower and have not been heard of since. I fear—I have been afraid for years that they are dead."

"Oh, Amrah," sobbed Ben-Hur. "This is a bitter homecoming!"

CHAPTER 7

Across the desert came a lone rider on a horse. He climbed several low hills, then descended into a large, circular plain neatly hidden from view.

The rider stopped before a cave in a hillside, and from out of the cave came a black-bearded man wearing a Roman breastplate over a Jewish tunic. The rider handed the man a letter.

As he read it, his cheeks flushed, and a wide grin spread across his face. "My friends," he called. "Our waiting is at an end!"

Several dark-haired, swarthy men, also dressed as the speaker, came out of the cave. "What does the letter say, Commander?" asked one of the men.

"It is from my friend Malluch in Antioch," said the first. "He says that a man called John has been proclaiming a coming king and that the king will come to Jerusalem very soon."

At this, a great cheer rose up from the men. Now the man with the letter said to the messenger, "Wait for me one moment. I will be with you again shortly." He quickly disappeared into the cave. A few minutes later, he came out with two letters and gave them to the messenger.

"Take these with great haste," he said. "One is to my servant Simonides in Antioch, the other to Sheik Ilderim."

The messenger bowed and then returned the way he had come.

Then the speaker said to two of his men, "Saddle my horse and get provisions ready for me. Tonight I ride to Jerusalem!"

The night was cold, clear, and dark. There was no moon to light the path of a traveler, only the star-speckled sky. Just the sort of night for a traveler wishing to go unseen.

Tonight the traveler was Ben-Hur. He spurred his horse southward across the wide desert. There was no road here. Few travelers except the desert jackal ever went this far north. Here an army could camp for years undiscovered.

An army did camp here. The camp lay in the hidden valley Ben-Hur had left just hours earlier. He had gathered ten thousand men from Galilee to prepare his army for the coming king. All through the winter months, he had trained the troops in the desert. He drilled them in the Roman legion's method of combat. Simonides bought the weapons and armor and horses; Sheik Ilderim and his people made sure no one discovered Ben-Hur's training camp.

The Galileans had proved eager for the task. Their hatred for Rome was even greater than their love for their own country. Of all the peoples of Israel they were the most fiercely independent, the most ready to revolt against Rome. As Ben-Hur went through their region telling of the coming king, more and more Galileans joined him.

They learned quickly. At the end of that spring, Ben-Hur felt his troops were ready.

And now this letter from Malluch! The king in Jerusalem could mean only one thing: He was ready to proclaim Himself. When He did, Ben-Hur would be there, ten thousand troops at his call.

They could easily crush any opposition in Jerusalem. Their success would bring many more thousands of Israelites to the new king's side. At last, Rome would meet an enemy more than its match!

Ben-Hur was still on the desert when dawn came. He stopped to rest his horse. In the growing light, he saw a camel in the distance, coming toward him. On the camel's back was a square tent of cloth.

The camel stopped before Ben-Hur. The tent flap was drawn aside, and there sat the old Egyptian, Balthasar.

"I give you God's greetings, son of Hur," said the Egyptian.

"The peace of the Lord to you," said Ben-Hur, bowing. "I am soon coming to a small stream where there are trees and soft grass. Please join me."

"I thank you. Lead on, and I will follow."

In about two hours they came to the stream, where they rested on the grass. Ben-Hur wanted to hear more about the Messiah, the coming king. He showed Balthasar the letter from Malluch.

Balthasar's face seemed to brighten as he read it. Then he closed his eyes and lifted his hands. "You have been very good to me, O God," he said. "Let me, I pray, see your savior just once more that I might worship Him again before I die."

Suddenly Ben-Hur remembered, or thought he remembered, something Balthasar had said in the office of Simonides a year ago: "He has come to save men's souls, not to save Israel from Rome."

Ben-Hur frowned as he thought of this. "O noble Egyptian," he said, "do you still believe the Messiah's kingdom is not of this earth?"

"I do," said Balthasar.

Three days later, they came to Bethabara by the Jordan River. Colored booths and tents were set up all along the shore. People were everywhere. *What is going on?* wondered Ben-Hur. *A festival?*

A man in a coarse brown tunic and long, shaggy hair was speaking to a group of people by the shore. Ben-Hur stopped a man going by. "Who is that man by the shore?" he asked.

"He is called John," said the man. "John the Baptist."

Suddenly the man called John pointed up the river, where a man was walking toward them. He wore a white robe that was well worn and travel stained. His hair and beard were the color of chestnut. His figure was rugged, His hands thick and sinewy, but His manner was calm, peaceful. He walked slowly.

Balthasar was staring at the man as if in a trance. Ben-Hur's heart leaped. Why? What was there about the man? His eyes! They were clear as desert pools and seemed to hold all the light of the sun.

Then came John's voice. "Behold the Lamb of God, Who takes away the sin of the world!"

CHAPTER 8

A courier rode up to the house of Hur on the Via Dolorosa in Jerusalem. He gave a letter to the servant at the gate. "To the master of the house, Simonides, from the son of Hur," the courier said. The servant went quickly to the roof of the house, where Simonides and his daughter sat.

"Tell me," said Esther excitedly, "what does it say?" as her father read the letter.

"It says that the coming king is on his way now to Jerusalem!" said Simonides, his hand shaking. "And Ben-Hur has sent two legions of troops following. He himself will come here tonight. He says the king announced that He was going to Jerusalem, where everything the prophets had written would now come true."

The Hur house was filled with life once more. Simonides had bought it from Pontius Pilate and restored it to its original splendor. Simonides, his daughter, and the old Egyptian, Balthasar, had come to live there. And Amrah, to her delight and pride, was once again the chief maidservant.

It was the twenty-first day of March, three years after the Messiah had come to John at Bethabara. Ben-Hur had stayed in the desert, gathering and training troops and following the news of the coming king of Israel. For three years now, the king had been going all over Judea, proclaiming the kingdom of God. Everywhere there was great talk of the many miracles this king was doing. He made the blind see, the lame walk. He even raised the dead to life.

Ben-Hur had been very troubled when he had gone to Jerusalem to see this king three years ago. He had thought the king was going to take His throne then, but nothing happened. Ben-Hur returned to the desert angry and confused. What was the king waiting for?

As time went by, Ben-Hur wondered more and more whether Balthasar was right. Was the coming kingdom not of this world?

It had been a lonely, frustrating time of waiting for Ben-Hur. He had lost all hope that his mother and sister were alive. He would remain a fugitive as long as Gratus still lived in Rome. He was denied a peaceful life like other men, with a wife, a family, a home. His life was the desert. His days were filled with drilling troops and training for war. And more and more, the pretty face of Esther, the merchant's daughter, came to him in his dreams at night.

He came tonight to his father's house. He climbed the stairs to the roof, where the merchant and his daughter sat with Balthasar. He bowed to the three, and they exchanged greetings. Ben-Hur's gaze rested the longest on Esther, but when she blushed and dropped her eyes, he quickly turned away. He had not meant to stare at her. *How beautiful she has become!* he thought.

"I bring news of the king," he said, taking a seat. There was eagerness in his voice.

Just then Amrah appeared. "Dear Amrah," said Ben-Hur.

"Have you—have you heard anything of them?"

She shook her head quickly. Her hands played nervously with her shawl. She retreated into a shadow and sat down.

Ben-Hur was silent for a moment. He took steady, deep breaths, as if to control a sob.

"Tell us of the king," said Balthasar.

Ben-Hur looked at the old Egyptian. "Maybe you are right," he said. "Maybe this man is a savior, not a king."

He looked at Simonides. "He does not look like a king," said Ben-Hur. "And He does not travel like a king." Many, many days I have been among the crowds that follow Him. He travels with twelve men whom He calls disciples. They are not royalty, but fishermen, tax collectors, tillers of the soil. They own nothing, take nothing with them. They travel on foot in the desert and sleep in the open with no tent.

"And yet," he continued, "His power is greater than any man's on earth, greater than any king's! I have seen Him heal the sick with just a spoken word. I have seen Him make the dumb speak, the lame walk, the blind see. At the gates of Nain, He said to a dead boy, 'Get up,' and the boy woke from death! Just yesterday, on the road He said to a leper, 'Be clean,' and as I looked, the leper's skin cleared and restored itself, and he was whole."

A slight gasp came from the shadow where Amrah sat. No one saw her scurry down the stairs and out into the street.

"We sit in the desert and wait," continued Ben-Hur. "The Galileans grow restless. Their swords are burning in their hands. Tomorrow Jesus the Nazarene, He Who is said to be the coming king, will come to the temple here. Then we will know what sort of king He is."

"The Lord lives, and so do the words of the prophets," said Simonides. "Tomorrow will tell indeed."

Balthasar nodded, smiling.

That night Amrah hurried down the street and out of the city. She went down into the eastern valley. The dark green side of Mt. Olivet was dotted with white tents. Many people had come to Jerusalem for the Passover celebration, which was the next day.

She went past the garden of Gethsemane, past the tombs at the meeting of the Bethany roads, past the pool of Siloam, past the King's Garden, until she came to the Hill of Evil.

Many caves were cut into the hill. It was a forbidden place. Here lived—and died—the lepers. The Jewish law condemned lepers to live here. Anyone in Jerusalem who caught the disease must come to this hill to live out the rest of his miserable life. Food was brought near the hill daily from the city. The lepers would come down the hill, take what food they could, and return to their caves.

All through the night, Amrah sat at the bottom of this hill. When the sun topped the eastern slopes, she climbed up the path to the hill. She did not stop at the food-drop point but hurried on up the forbidden path until she came to a woman sitting in front of a cave.

The woman's face was uncovered. It was ghastly white and shriveled. On seeing Amrah, she threw her hood over her face. "Unclean! Unclean!" she cried. "Amrah! What are you doing? Have you lost your senses? You know the law. Oh, Amrah, now you cannot go back. You must remain here and die one of us!"

Amrah knelt to the ground. She was so excited she could barely speak. "Your son, Judah, was at the house last night," she said. "He told us of the man Who is called Jesus of Nazareth. This Jesus has the power to heal. He made a leper clean!"

Ben-Hur's mother stood up. She was shaking. "How does my son know this?" she asked.

"He has followed the Nazarene and has seen Him do these things," said Amrah. "The Nazarene is coming to Jerusalem today! He can heal you and Tirzah. Come! You must come with me to the road. We will wait for Him there."

Now Tirzah came out of the cave. "Who is this man Amrah speaks of, Mother?" she asked.

"If He does what Amrah says, He must be the Messiah," said the mother. "Many years ago the story went around that He was born in Bethlehem. I remember it well. That must have been thirty years ago; He would be a man by now. Could it be He?"

"It is said that the Nazarene was born in Bethlehem," said Amrah. "Everyone is talking of Him. When your son spoke of Him last night, suddenly hope sprang up in my heart. You can be made well—I believe it! Come. We must hurry!"

Trembling, the mother turned to Tirzah. "Let us go," she said.

The three picked their way among the rocks covering the western slope of the hill, Tirzah and her mother moving very slowly. In the three years since their deliverance from the dungeon, the disease had eaten all through their bodies, leaving them more dead than alive. Their limbs were like those of skeletons, their faces like those of hideous ancient hags.

When they reached the bottom of the hill, they slumped to the grass by the side of the road.

It was nearly three years ago that Amrah had heard the news of the release of prisoners from the dungeons. The message had come to her one night that two women, lepers, had gone from the city to the lepers' colony. Amrah had gone there and found them, but Ben-Hur's mother had pleaded with Amrah not to tell her son where they were. "If he knew we were lepers, he would come here and die with us," his mother said. So Amrah had kept their secret, coming to the hill daily with food for them. Every time Ben-Hur came to the house to visit, he asked of his mother and sister, and every time Amrah had to lie and say she had not heard anything, though her heart nearly broke.

Now as the three women waited by the road, Amrah's joy was nearly complete. First Ben-Hur had returned, and now, very soon, his mother and sister would be whole again.

Soon people started coming down the road from the city. They came shouting and waving palm branches. More and more came shouting, "Hosanna! Hosanna to the king!"

And then the king came from the other direction, riding a donkey. A huge crowd came with Him, shouting and dancing.

"These two crowds will meet right here," said Tirzah. "The master will never hear us call to Him in all this noise."

The crowds did meet right there. Thousands of people shouted praises to God while Ben-Hur's mother fell on her knees and clasped her hands.

The Nazarene seemed unaware of all the people and the clamor. He was looking at Tirzah and her mother. He rode up to them.

Suddenly people noticed the lepers. "The lepers!" they screamed. "Kill them! Stone them!" Several people began picking up stones to throw. The Nazarene simply held up His hand, and the people stopped as though struck.

"O Master!" cried Tirzah's mother. "You see our need. You can make us clean. Have mercy on us."

"Do you believe I am able to do this?" He asked.

"You are He of Whom the prophets spoke," she answered. "You are the Messiah!"

He smiled. In that smile was the look of a loving father and a powerful king. "Your faith is great," He said. "It is done for you, just as you believe." He stared at them a moment longer, then turned back to the road.

Slowly the crowds passed. Before the last had gone by, the miracle was complete. The women felt a tingling start deep in their bones, then spread throughout their bodies. As Amrah stood speechless, the two women were transformed before her eyes.

Now the crowds had passed. Only one man was still walking down the road. The three women were hugging and weeping and praising God. The man came closer.

"Mother!" cried the man. "And Tirzah!"

"Judah! My son!"

Ben-Hur had been following the crowd into the city. Farther behind, yet unseen, were two legions of his Galilean troops. And there before him stood his mother and sister. They were just as he remembered them, so long ago. His mother had a few strands of gray in her hair now, though her face seemed just as young. And Tirzah was a woman now, even more beautiful than he remembered.

Now mother, son, and daughter embraced and wept and laughed. And as Ben-Hur wept, all the years of bitterness, of pain, of hate, of desire for revenge, washed off of him like dirt in a gentle rain.

Two days later, the crowds had gathered again. Thousands and thousands of people seethed around a hill called Golgotha, but now there were no shouts of praise to God, no singing, no laughter.

The Nazarene hung from a tall wooden cross on top of the hill. Two other crosses were there, from which hung two common criminals. From the masses of people came taunts and curses and screams of hatred.

A crown of thorns encircled the Nazarene's head. Blood covered Him, head to foot. An inscription above Him read, "Jesus Christ, the king of the Jews."

In the vast crowd stood Ben-Hur, his mother and sister, Balthasar, and Esther. Simonides sat propped up in a litter raised on supports.

What had happened? How had the crowds turned so suddenly, so viciously, against their king? The twelve disciples had deserted Jesus; the Galilean troops had deserted Ben-Hur. The hatred of the Jews for this Nazarene was unimaginable. He had come to their cities and spoken of a new kingdom. He had said, "I am the bread of life. Anyone who comes to Me will never again be hungry. I am the resurrection and the life. No one comes to the Father but by Me."

He had healed the sick, cast out demons, made the blind see, the lame walk. He had raised the dead. Thousands and thousands from all over had called Him the King, the Messiah, the Son of God.

And now He hung dying on a cross.

Tears poured down Balthasar's face. Simonides stared vacantly. Esther shook with sobbing. She looked at Ben-Hur.

"Is it still too late?" she asked. "Can you not save Him?"

Ben-Hur's face was strangely peaceful. He shook his head sadly. "He has all the power of God at His command," he said. "He could save Himself if He wished. This is as He wills it."

Balthasar nodded. "O Lord!" he said. "To think that I would live to see this horrible day! This is the day of damnation, the day of darkness." He closed his eyes and raised his tear-streaked face to heaven. "Yet I know that He will rise," he said. "On the third day He will rise, as it is written. And He will live and will rule. And His kingdom will last forever and ever. It is written."

And now the tears came pouring down Simonides' face. "Ah, dear God in heaven!" he said. "I see at last. I believe. You are the Son of God!"

"Yes, Lord," said Ben-Hur, "Your kingdom is not of this world."

Suddenly the sky grew dark. The crowd grew deathly quiet.

The darkness hung over the land for three hours. Then Jesus cried out, "It is finished!" His head dropped to His chest. Then the ground began to tremble, and the crowds began to scream and run. They went stumbling over the rolling ground, screaming, weeping, tearing their hair, beating their breasts.

But Ben-Hur's group stood still with raised arms and praised God in tearful voices. Ben-Hur put his arms around Esther, and they worshipped God together.

He had found peace at last. He had found his mother and sister. He had found his love, the beautiful Esther. And he had found his king. He could see the kingdom now—could feel it. It was rich and vast and growing, growing, growing. It was in his heart.

THE PILGRIM'S PROGRESS

PART ONE

by John Bunyan
retold by Dan Larsen

Introduction

Part One of John Bunyan's *Pilgrim's Progress* was first published in 1678. Part Two followed six years later. This book has been read by more people than any other book except the Bible. It is among the greatest books on earth.

The Pilgrim's Progress is actually two stories. Part One is about Christian, who takes a long journey to the holy city. On the way, he meets enough danger and adventure to turn any man back, but he must go on. Part Two tells the story of Christiana, Christian's wife. She, too, finds that she must make the same journey.

Here are tall mountains and dark valleys, great heroes and evil giants. Here, too, are ordinary men and women, who together face the perils of the pilgrim's journey.

This story is an allegory. That means that the names of certain people and places not only describe those people and places, but also stand for something else more significant. Christian, for instance, is the story's hero. Yet his name also stands for every person who decides to follow Jesus Christ.

In that sense, this story is not make-believe. It is very real. Christian follows the same straight, narrow path through the wilderness that every Christian travels in his or her own journey through life.

And the end of the journey is just as magnificent in real life as it is in *The Pilgrim's Progress*.

CHAPTER 1

The man stood in the field outside the City of Destruction and cried out in terror, "What shall I do?"

His clothes were ragged, and his back was bowed as if with a heavy load on his shoulders. He was reading a book, and what he read made him weep and tremble. His name was Christian.

That night at home, he tried to hide his anguish from his family but could not. He burst out, "We are doomed! I have learned that unless we escape this city, we will all be burned by fire from heaven."

His wife and sons were astonished. "You have taken a fever," said his wife. "Go to bed now. Sleep will settle your wits."

But Christian could not sleep. He tossed and he turned. In the morning he said, "I am worse yet. And this burden is even heavier."

And this went on for many days.

Christian's friends, even his family, scorned him. "He has gone out of his mind!" they said.

So he spent his days alone, walking in the fields, reading in his book, sometimes praying, sometimes weeping. One day, as he stood reading he cried, "What shall I do to be saved?"

Just as he said this a man, tall and strong, walked up to him. "My name is Evangelist," said the man. "What troubles you so?"

"Oh, Sir," said Christian. "I have read here that because of the bad things I have done, I will die and be punished forever."

Evangelist then handed Christian a roll of paper. On it was written, "Flee from the wrath to come."*

"Which way?" cried Christian.

"Follow the light there," said Evangelist, pointing across a wide field. "You will come to a wicket gate. Knock at the gate, and you will be told what to do."

Christian saw a light shining far away, where the man pointed. Now he began running toward it. At last he felt some hope.

"Come back, Fool!" came a cry from behind. Now two men from the city, whose names were Obstinate and Pliable, caught up with Christian and grabbed him by the arm.

"We saw you running away," they said. "We have come to bring you back."

"Never!" said Christian. "You live in the City of Destruction, which will be destroyed by fire. I go to find life."

And Christian told them of things promised in the book he had, of a life that lasts forever, a life free to all who flee the coming destruction.

"You have lost your wits, crazy fool!" said Obstinate, and he turned back.

But Pliable said, "If this life indeed be true, then I would seek it with you."

And so they set out together.

---

*Matthew 3:7

As they walked, Christian read to Pliable from the book, about an everlasting kingdom where the righteous would live forever. "Then shall the righteous shine forth as the sun in the kingdom of their Father."*

The men grew eager for these things. And as their eagerness grew, they began to fear that something evil was following them and would catch them before they reached this kingdom. They began to run.

Suddenly they tumbled into a bog and began to sink. Pliable struggled desperately to the side and dragged himself out. "So! This is the life your good book promises," he snarled. "Well, not for me!" And he turned back to the city.

Christian sank deeper in the mire. The load on his back was dragging him under. Just as the bog closed over his head, he felt a strong hand grab his arm, and he was pulled out onto dry ground.

Christian stood dripping filthy mud and looked into the kind face of his rescuer.

"My name is Help," said the man. "This bog is called the Slough of Despond. It is the dumping place of all the fears and doubts of people who are lost in sin. If you look hard, you will see steps through it that the King has placed here. But watch carefully!"

Christian did watch carefully then and crossed the bog safely. As he went on, he met another man, Mr. Worldly Wiseman from the Town of Carnal.

---

*Matthew 13:43

"And where are you going, and why so bent over as if with a heavy load?" asked the man.

Christian told him of his journey and of the man, Evangelist, who sent him.

"Fah!" said Wiseman. "Evangelist! His is the hardest road to follow. Come, I will show you a way that is easy, and where many pleasures await you."

Mr. Wiseman pointed to a high hill, where lived Mr. Legality in the city of Morality. "His is the first house you come to. He will ease that burden off you."

Christian eagerly set out for this hill. But as he started to climb, his burden grew heavier and heavier. Then suddenly, flames shot out at him from the hill. He fell down in terror.

"Christian! Why have you come this way?" came a voice. There stood Evangelist, untouched by the flames as they lashed around him.

So Christian told him of Mr. Worldly Wiseman and Mr. Legality.

Evangelist said, "Listen to what the Lord says: 'Strive to enter in at the strait gate: for many, I say unto you, will seek to enter in, and shall not be able.'* All other ways lead to death. Mr. Legality only leads you away from the one place where you can leave your burden, which is your sins. That place is the Cross."

---

*Luke 13:24

Christian repented for having turned out of the way. He felt ashamed for having taken Mr. Worldly Wiseman's advice. Now he went along, not speaking to anyone he met, until finally he reached the wicket gate. Over the gate was written, "Knock, and it shall be opened unto you."* So Christian knocked.

Soon a man came to the gate. "I am Goodwill," he said. "What do you wish here?"

"Sir," said Christian, "I came from the City of Destruction to escape the wrath that is coming, and I want to know if you are willing to let me in."

"With all my heart," said Goodwill.

But as Christian stepped up to the doorway, Goodwill quickly grabbed him and pulled him through. Goodwill pointed to a dark castle on a nearby mountain. "That is the castle of Beelzebub," he said. "The evil beings there shoot arrows at those who try to enter here."

Now Goodwill asked Christian of his journey. Christian told him of the troubles he had met with on the way, of Pliable and how he had turned back, of the city of Morality and the hill where Mr. Legality lived, and of the fire that stopped him from going farther.

"That hill has brought the death of many who turned

*Matthew 7:7

aside," said Goodwill. "But happily you have escaped. Now, look. There is your road," he said, pointing to a straight, narrow path. "There are many turnings, wide and crooked, but your way must always be on the straight and narrow.

"Go now," Goodwill said. "Soon you will come to the house of the Interpreter. He will help you understand many things about your journey here."

"Sir," said Christian, "I still carry this burden. Will you help me off with it?"

"You must carry that yet," said Goodwill, "until you come to the Cross."

Then Christian said good-bye to Goodwill and started on the narrow road. Soon he came to the house of the Interpreter and knocked on the door.

"Come in," said the Interpreter. "I will show you things that you will need to know."

The Interpreter lit a candle and led Christian into a parlor where the floor was covered with dust. A man came in and began to sweep. As he swept, the dust flew about the room so that Christian could hardly breathe.

"Now bring the water," said the Interpreter. A girl entered, sprinkled water about the room, then swept it clean.

"Now I will tell you what this means," said the Interpreter. "This parlor is the heart of a person lost in sin. The dust is his sin. The sweeper is the Law, which stirs up but can not clean. The water is the gospel, which washes the heart clean."

Then the Interpreter brought Christian to a fireplace. A man stood there in a rage, throwing buckets of water on the fire. But with each dash of water, the fire only burned brighter.

Now the Interpreter took Christian behind the wall, where a man stood throwing fuel on the fire.

"What does all this mean?" asked Christian.

"This fire is the work of grace in a person's heart," said the Interpreter. "The man trying to quench the fire is the devil. The man fueling the fire is Christ, Who always keeps alive every work He begins in a person's heart."

The Interpreter showed Christian many other things before he sent him on his way again. "Never let anyone lead you off the path," said the Interpreter. "Their way leads to death. And remember, the Comforter, God's own spirit, will guide you through any hard places you come to on your journey."

CHAPTER 3

Christian left the house of the Interpreter and started up the narrow road. His going was slow because of the load on his back.

Before long he came to a grassy hill. On it stood a wooden cross. Christian stopped. He stared in wonder at the cross. Suddenly, the heavy load on his back slid off and tumbled downhill. His burden was gone!

Christian felt so light! Tears filled his eyes as he thought of the one Who had hung on that cross for him. "He has taken my heavy load by His sorrow," Christian said, weeping.

As he stood there, three men appeared. They shone like the sun.

"Peace to you," said the first. "Your sins are forgiven."

The second gave Christian new white clothing.

The third gave him a roll of paper. "This is written for you," he said. "It will bring help to you when you are troubled."

Now the three men left Christian. He quickly took off his old, ragged clothes and put on the clean, new ones. Then he gave a leap of joy and sang a song of praise to the one Who had taken his burden.

He went on his way. On either side of the road was a wall, called Salvation. Christian had not gone far when two men climbed over the wall onto the road just ahead. Their names were Formalist and Hypocrisy.

"Ho, there!" called Christian. "Where are you going?"

"To Mount Zion," they said, "where we will find glory for ourselves."

"Why did you not come in at the gate?" asked Christian. "It is written, 'He that entereth not by the door into the sheepfold, but climbeth up some other way, the same is a thief and a robber.' "*

"Bah!" they said. "That way is much too hard. We chose an easier way."

"But won't the Lord of the City call you trespassers when you come there, if you were not invited in at the gate?" said Christian.

"You were invited," they sneered. "We climbed in. Now we are both here, and how are you better than we?"

"I am a guest here," said Christian. "You are trespassers."

They laughed at him at this. Christian went ahead on his way, and they followed. Now the road went up a steep hill called Difficulty. At the bottom was a spring. Christian drank deeply. Feeling refreshed, he started the long climb.

But the two men behind him turned away when they got to the hill. "Why bother with this long, hard climb?" they said. "Let us find an easier way."

But as they went, they got separated. One wandered lost in a dark forest called Danger, the other in the Mountains of Destruction. They were never seen again.

The Hill of Difficulty was so steep that Christian had to climb on his hands and knees. About halfway up, he came to a level spot with a shady bower set up for weary travelers.

*John 10:1

Exhausted, he lay down and fell asleep. The sun dropped in the sky, the day passed, and still he slept.

As he dreamed, a hand shook him and a voice said, "Go to the ant, thou sluggard; consider her ways, and be wise.* Awake!"

Christian, startled awake, climbed the rest of the way up the hill. Then he went on.

Suddenly he froze. From somewhere ahead came a scream of terror. Then two men, Timorous and Mistrust, burst past him and scrambled down the hill he had just climbed.

"Go back!" they cried, "Two huge beasts lie on the path before you! They will tear you to pieces!"

Trembling, Christian peered ahead in the growing darkness. What should he do now?

Suddenly Christian remembered the roll of paper the shining man had given him. "It will help you in your troubles," he had said. Christian reached for it. But it was gone!

Horrors! thought Christian. He must have dropped it on his climb. The only thing to do now was turn back. He slowly, painfully climbed down the hill. As he went he searched for the roll. "Oh, why did I sleep?" he moaned. "Now I am done!"

At last he came to the bower, and there on the ground was the roll! Now he felt new strength. He began the climb again.

But by the time he reached the top, night had fallen. And the beasts lay ahead! Clutching his roll tightly, he walked on in the darkness. *The wild beasts hunt at night,* he thought. *This is the end of me!*

---

*Proverbs 6:6

Just then a huge shape loomed out of the darkness. Terrified, Christian could only stare at it, waiting. Then he realized what it was. A castle. Maybe he could stay here tonight.

But as he went forward, he saw just ahead, on either side of the road, two huge lions, still as statues. Christian turned to run. But a voice stopped him.

"Do not fear the lions! They are chained. They are there to turn back those who have no faith. Stay in the middle of the path, and you will not be harmed."

Christian crept past the lions as he was told. Though they roared terribly, they could not reach him.

Soon he was past them. He came to the castle.

"I am Watchful, the porter," said the voice. "This house was built by the lord of the hill. It is for the rest and safety of weary pilgrims. Welcome."

The porter brought Christian into the castle. There he met three sisters, Prudence, Piety, and Charity. They brought some food and sat down to eat with Christian.

As they ate, they talked about his journey and the people he had met. Then they talked of the Lord of the hill, the one Who had built that castle. The Lord, said the sisters, had made princes of many poor pilgrims. And because of His great love, He had died on a cross for them. They talked late into the night.

Christian rested there for several days. When the time came for him to leave, the sisters brought him some weapons that the Lord had made: a sword, a shield, a helmet, a breastplate, a belt, and shoes that never wore out.

"These are for your protection against any evil you meet on your way," the sisters said. "Good-bye, Christian."

Chapter 4

Now Christian's way went down into the Valley of Humiliation. He passed slowly through meadows and fields of lilies. Then suddenly, the sun was blotted out for an instant.

Christian looked, just in time to see a huge monster drop out of the sky onto the road. The monster was covered with scales. He had wings like a dragon's, feet like a bear's, and a head like a lion's. He breathed fire and smoke.

"I am Apollyon," the beast said. "Where do you come from, and where are you going?"

"I come from the City of Destruction and am going to the City of Zion," said Christian, his voice trembling.

"You are from my country," said Apollyon, "I am the prince and god of that place. You are in my service. Do not go any farther. You must return."

"I serve another prince now, evil one," said Christian. "And I will not turn back!"

At this, a wicked light flared in Apollyon's eyes. He spread his wings. "You will die here!" he screamed.

He hurled fiery darts at Christian, one after another. Christian stopped the darts with his shield and drew his sword. He fought back with all his strength.

The battle lasted for hours. Christian was bloodied and weary. Finally he stumbled, and the sword flew out of his hand. In a flash, Apollyon was on him. But Christian grabbed his sword and thrust upward furiously—and his blade struck scaly flesh!

Apollyon screamed in pain. He flew off, spouting fire and blood. The battle was over.

Christian sank to the ground, praising the Lord. "In all these things we are more than conquerors through him that loved us," he said.*

Now as he lay panting and bleeding, a hand appeared holding leaves from the Tree of Life. The hand touched his wounds. They were healed instantly.

Now as Christian went, he kept his sword in his hand. He crossed the valley with no more trouble.

But as night fell, he came to another valley. This was the Valley of the Shadow of Death. What Christian saw before him made a cold sweat break out on his forehead.

The road was very narrow here. On one side was a ditch that looked bottomless. On the other was a black, evil smelling swamp. Here Christian's sword would do no good. He prayed aloud as he went forward.

Now from out of the pit came fire that licked across the path.

Now from out of the night came terrible voices. All around him they howled and screamed.

The voices, like demons from hell, came nearer and nearer. At last Christian cried, "I will walk in the strength of the Lord!" Suddenly the night was still. And Christian went on.

---

*Romans 8:37

CHAPTER 5

Morning came. Christian had passed through the valley. Now he turned to look back. In the morning light, he saw clearly the place he had gone through. "Only by the Lord's strength!" he said, "turneth the shadow of death into the morning."*

The road now went up out of the valley. As Christian climbed, he saw someone ahead of him. It was Faithful, a man from Christian's city. Christian called to him and ran to catch up with him.

The two went on together, glad of each other's company on so lonely and difficult a journey.

"I would have followed you when you fled the city," said Faithful. "But you were too far ahead of me. So I came this way alone. Though everyone there was talking fearfully of the city's being burned, no one would come with me."

And Christian and Faithful talked of their journeys.

Faithful told Christian of the many people he had met, all of whom had tried to make him turn back. Some of their names he remembered: Deceit. Discontent. Shame. Pride. Arrogance.

"What did you say to them?" asked Christian.

"That nothing they could say, no riches they could promise, would make me go back," said Faithful, "because this is the path the Lord has set for me. I told them that a poor man

---

*Amos 5:8

who loves Christ is richer by far than the greatest man in the world who hated Him. And I told them that those who become fools for the kingdom of heaven are the wisest of all."

Then Christian told Faithful of his many adventures.

Soon they saw a man ahead of them. He was tall and from a distance looked handsome. But as they came up to him, Faithful saw something in his face that he did not like.

"Hello," said Faithful to the stranger. "Are you going to the heavenly country?"

"I am," said the man.

"Then let us go together," said Faithful.

"Very good. As we go, we can talk of good things. And what better things are there to talk of than God?"

"I begin to like you very much, Friend," said Faithful.

As they talked, Faithful grew amazed at the man's knowledge of things good and evil.

But now Christian pulled Faithful aside. "Do you not know who this is?" he asked. "His name is Talkative. He comes from our own city. He speaks fine words and likes to appear a friend to everyone. But those who know him are afraid to turn their backs to him. He is full of lies and trickery. He preaches religion in his church, but among the drunken thieves at the ale house he is the worst. Beware of him!"

Faithful was astonished at hearing this. "But he speaks truthfully of the kingdom of heaven, of the Good Book, and of the religion," he said.

"His religion is on his tongue, not in his heart," said Christian. "People say of him, 'a saint abroad, and a devil at home.' Remember, saying is not the same thing as doing."

"I believe you, my friend," said Faithful. "I will test this man with a question."

So he said to Talkative, "Sir, tell me. What proof is there of a work of grace in a person's heart?"

"Great knowledge of the gospel," said Talkative, proudly.

"But a person can have great knowledge and still no change in his soul," said Faithful. "You cannot please God with knowledge only. You must obey Him. Remember, the psalmist wrote, 'Teach me, O LORD, the way of thy statutes; and I shall keep it unto the end.' "*

Faithful went on. "Another proof of grace in the heart is the sorrow and shame that come on a person for the evil things he has done. And if a person leaves his sins at the cross, the one Who died there and rose again will give him joy and peace in place of his sorrow.

"Have you done this, Talkative?" asked Faithful. "Can your religion stand this test?"

Talkative's face flushed. His eyes darted nervously. "Why are you asking me this?" he said.

"Because I have heard of you," said Faithful. "I know that outside you look clean, but inside you are full of dirt."

Talkative turned and stalked away. "You are not fit to talk to!" he snapped.

"His loss is no one's fault but his own," said Christian. "You did the best thing you could for him. You told him the truth."

---

*Psalm 119:33

CHAPTER 6

The road now led Christian and Faithful through a wilderness of forests and mountains. Here they met the one who had shown each of them the way to the gate, Evangelist.

"Welcome, my good friend," said Christian.

"A thousand welcomes," said Faithful.

"And how has it been with you since we last spoke?" asked Evangelist.

So they told him of all the dangers and hardships they had gone through.

"I am glad that you have been victorious in these things," said Evangelist. "Do not lose heart. A crown awaits each of you at the end of your journey here. Now you must hear what I have to say. Soon you will come to a town. You will be taken by enemies. There you must give testimony to the truth. One of you will lose your life for your faith. But that one will gain his reward in the eternal city sooner than the other."

Then Evangelist embraced them and left. They continued on their way in silence, each thinking about what Evangelist had told them.

Very soon, they came to a town called Vanity. This town was built by Beelzebub and Apollyon. There were many things bought and sold there. And many evil men—thieves, murderers, swindlers—lived there.

As Christian and Faithful walked down the street, they drew

many stares. All along the street were carts of sellers loaded with everything imaginable. Many of the sellers jeered at the two men. Many more called out for them to buy something.

A fat, unshaven man spat at Faithful's foot and sneered. "What'll you buy, stranger?" he said.

"We buy only the truth," said Faithful.

The two friends met many more men like this. As the day went on, a crowd gathered against them. "We must destroy these two," they whispered.

Christian and Faithful were grabbed and taken to the lord of the town.

"What do you mean, causing trouble in our town?" demanded the lord. "Who are you, and what do you want here?"

"We are just passing through here, Sir," said Faithful. "And there has been no trouble here of our making."

The lord could tell by the men's clothes and weapons that they were pilgrims. And he knew that pilgrims brought only trouble to his town. So he had them locked up in a cage and set in the street where everyone mocked them.

But Christian and Faithful kept quiet and did not return the insults to their tormentors.

Now there were a few in that town not so bad as the rest. These began arguing with the others, saying they should let the men go. The argument became a fight, and soon the whole street was in chaos.

Now the lord of the town was furious. He had the two men beaten and locked in irons. "You will die for this latest trouble you have caused!" he said.

But they did not say a word.

The men were brought to trial. They were charged with being enemies to the town's trade of selling and with causing a dangerous division among the men at the fair.

"These things are against the laws of our prince, Beelzebub," said the judge, whose name was Lord Hate-good.

Faithful answered, "We are men of peace and do not make trouble. Those men who came to our defense did so because they believed we were in truth and innocence. And as for your lord, Beelzebub, I defy him. He is the enemy of our Lord."

Three men from the fair, Envy, Superstition, and Pickthank, took the stand and accused Faithful of many things.

"This man is against all our customs," they said. "He has spoken evil of our lord and our town. He said Christianity and our law stood against each other, that our religion is evil, and that our noble prince, Beelzebub, belongs in hell with other enemies of this man's god."

"Sirs," said Faithful, "I have said no wicked things to anyone. I have spoken only the truth. The truth is, your laws are wrong if they stand against the Word of God. And anyone who follows your prince, Beelzebub, is himself an enemy of God."

For this, Faithful was condemned. He was dragged outside, whipped, and beaten until he died.

But just as the crowd of men were about to cheer at his death, they gasped. A chariot, drawn by two horses, rose up into the sky carrying Faithful.

"Blessed Faithful!" cried Christian. "Though they killed you, you are alive!"

After Faithful's death, Christian was locked in the cage again. There he awaited his own trial. But one night an angel came, broke the cage door open, and led Christian out of town.

Christian gave thanks to the Lord and ran as far away as possible from that evil place. The next day, he woke and started on his way. He heard a cry from behind and turned to look.

A man came running up. "I am from Vanity," he said. "My name is now Hopeful, because by your friend's faith and yours, you gave me hope. I wish to go with you to the Celestial City. And there are many more like me in the town who, sooner or later, will take this road, too."

"My friend died for his faith," said Christian. "You have risen from his ashes and are now my companion. Welcome, Friend."

They embraced and set out together.

About midday, Christian and Hopeful came to a small hill called Lucre. In that hill was a silver mine. In front of the mine stood a man who called to them.

"Ho, gentlemen," he said. "Come! I wish to show you something. In this mine is a treasure in silver. For a little digging, you can be rich men."

"Let us go see!" said Hopeful. He started to go.

"No!" said Christian, grabbing Hopeful. "I have heard of

this place. Many have gone to this mine seeking treasure and have fallen into a pit, never to be heard of again. This man leads men to their deaths."

"Demas!" Christian called. "You are an enemy of the Lord's. Your father was Judas, the traitor, and you are no better than he. Be assured that when we come to the King, He will hear of you!"

And they left him.

Soon the two men came to a beautiful river. On the banks were soft meadows and many fruit trees. King David had called this place the River of God. John the Baptist called it the River of Living Water.

No evil could live in this place. The men rested here for several days, drinking from the river and eating fruit from the trees. When they were refreshed, they went on their way.

It was not long, though, before the road grew rough and rocky. They began wishing they had stayed by the river.

Soon the road went past a smooth meadow. Christian said, "Look. There is a path in this meadow that runs alongside the road. It would be much nicer to walk there."

So they crawled over the wall that ran alongside the road and went on in the meadow. Just then they saw a man walking ahead on the path.

Christian and Hopeful called to the man. "Sir, where does this path lead?" they asked.

"To the Celestial City," he said. "I am Vain-confidence. Come. Follow me."

"Did I not tell you?" said Christian to Hopeful. "We are

on the right path."

They followed the man for a few hours, until night fell. Soon it grew very dark. They lost sight of Vain-confidence.

Suddenly came a scream. Then all was silent. The two friends crept forward in terror.

"Stop!" cried Christian. In front of their feet gaped a dark pit. They could not see the bottom. "He must have fallen here," said Christian.

Now it began to rain. Then thunder boomed and lightning flashed.

"Oh, why did we go off the road!" cried Hopeful.

The men wandered in the storm, seeking shelter. At last they found a dry bank under a large rock. They crawled in and fell asleep.

That night Christian had evil dreams. He dreamed that he and Hopeful were lost at sea in a storm. The rain beat down on their heads, and the waves smashed them about.

He cried out in his sleep, "Forgive me, Lord, for turning out of the way! Do not let us drown here!"

Outside their rock shelter, the rain pounded down and floodwaters rose. The men slept on.

"Awake!" came a terrible voice. Christian and Hopeful were jolted awake. Before them in the pouring rain stood a huge, grizzled giant.

"This is my land!" he bellowed. "No man comes here!"

The giant, whose name was Despair, drove them before him to his home called Doubting Castle. There he took them down a long flight of stone steps and threw them into a dark, foul smelling dungeon. They heard a key turn in the rusty lock.

Then all was silent.

Many days went by as the two friends sat together in the dark dungeon. They grew weaker and weaker.

Suddenly one day the lock clicked, the heavy door swung open, and there stood the giant. In his hand was a massive club. He lurched into the room and viciously beat the men. Then he was gone, laughing.

Christian and Hopeful had never felt such despair! That night they prayed to God. They had prayed almost the whole night through when suddenly Christian jumped up.

"What a fool I am to have forgotten!" he said. "Look! I have a key called Promise that will open any door of Doubting Castle." Quickly, he tried it in the lock. The door swung open!

The men climbed the stairs and ran to the outer door. It, too, opened to Christian's key. They were free!

They ran and ran until they came to the road again.

CHAPTER 8

After their escape from Doubting Castle, the two friends were hungry, tired, and still sore from their beating. They went slowly along the narrow road.

Soon the road began climbing into some mountains. When the pilgrims reached the top of the first mountain, they found a beautiful land before them. Here were gardens, orchards, vineyards, and fountains of clear, sparkling water. The weary pilgrims ate and drank and rested.

As they walked about here, they came on a group of shepherds tending sheep. The pilgrims asked the shepherds what mountains these were.

"These are the Delectable Mountains," said one shepherd. "These, and the sheep on them, belong to the Lord. We are within sight of His city here."

Then the shepherds, whose names were Knowledge, Experience, Watchful, and Sincere, asked the men about themselves. And when the shepherds learned the men were travelers to the holy city, they said, "Welcome."

The shepherds invited Christian and Hopeful into their tents and shared their food and drink with them.

"You may stay here and rest from your travels," the shepherds said. "The Lord has made these mountains for travelers such as you. You may sleep in our tents tonight. Tomorrow we will show you some wonders in these mountains."

So the next day, the shepherds took them to the top of a mountain named Caution. "Look down into the valley," said one shepherd.

The two friends looked and saw, far away, men wandering blindly among tombstones. The men seemed lost and sometimes stumbled over the tombstones.

"These men you see are ones who got off the narrow road, thinking they had found an easier way," said a shepherd. "They were caught by Giant Despair. That wicked giant put out their eyes and left them here to wander around forever."

After this, the shepherds took Christian and Hopeful down a mountainside, deep into a dark ravine. On one side of the ravine was a blackened, ancient door.

"Look inside," said a shepherd.

Cautiously, Christian opened the door, and the two men peered inside. At first they could see nothing. But as they looked, they began to see a fire burning, far away, deep under the mountain.

Then came a smell of bitter smoke.

Then came deep rumbling sounds.

Then came horrible cries of agony and terror.

The men shuddered as they quickly shut the door.

"This is a doorway to hell," said a shepherd. "There are many such doors. But this one is where liars and traitors enter. Here went Esau, who sold the birthright the Lord gave him. And here went Judas, who sold the Son of God."

Christian and Hopeful looked at each other grimly.

The shepherds then brought the two friends to the top of

another mountain called Clear.

One shepherd took a looking glass out of his cloak and handed it to Christian. "Here you can see the gates of the Celestial City—if your hand is steady enough to hold this looking glass."

Christian looked. He was still shaken by what he had seen and heard through that doorway. His hands trembled, and he could see nothing. He held on and gripped tighter. At last he caught a glimpse of a magnificent pair of gates. The sight was enough to ease his troubled heart.

Hopeful looked next, and he, too, thought he saw the gates.

Now the shepherds led them out of the mountains. As they said good-bye, one shepherd handed Christian a note. "Read this when you need instructions," he said. "And beware of the false one and of the Enchanted Ground."

CHAPTER 9

As Christian and Hopeful went down out of the Delectable Mountains, they sang for joy. They had seen the gates of the City! The end of their journey was near.

The going was easy for a little way. The road went past green meadows and forests.

Soon, though, it cut between two rugged cliffs. The pass was so narrow that the men had to walk one in front of the other. The cliffs blotted out all sunlight. The men went cautiously.

Christian stopped. "I hear something coming!" he whispered. Though they could not tell why, the two friends were afraid. They hid behind a large rock.

Suddenly down the path shuffled a group of tall, wiry-haired beasts carrying a bundle that struggled furiously. The beasts had long arms, wicked teeth, and horns on their heads. They carried a man bound with ropes. He writhed in their grasp and begged for mercy.

Now the beasts turned off the path. And Christian noticed a sign strapped to the man's back. It read Apostate (to turn away from faith in God). Then it seemed that the beasts disappeared right into the side of the cliff!

When Christian and Hopeful finally dared to come out, they crept to the place where the beasts had disappeared. There they saw a narrow cleft in the wall. They went to it and peered in.

This was another passage between two cliffs. Ahead on this path was the group of beasts. Then one of them opened a door in the cliff, and they all entered. The two men then recognized the door. It was the entrance to hell!

Christian and Hopeful got out of that dark place as fast as they could. As they went, they prayed they would meet nothing else on that terrible path.

Soon after the men were out of that passage, they came to a fork in the road. Both roads went up a hill. Neither was straighter than the other.

"Which way do we go?" cried Hopeful. "The roads look the same."

As they were talking about this, a man came to them. He was wearing a white robe with a hood. The two friends could not see his face.

"If you seek the way to the Celestial City, follow me," he said.

They gladly followed him. Their way went through a dense forest. As the road climbed, it gradually began to turn. The men did not notice this turning. They were busy picking their way through the briars and thorns that now reached out of the woods across the path. These grew thicker and thicker. Soon the men could go no farther.

Suddenly a net dropped over them. They were caught fast!

The figure in front of Christian and Hopeful then threw off his robe. He was covered with black hair. He laughed through gleaming teeth, then disappeared into the dark woods.

The two men could barely move. They struggled with the

net, but it was no use. "We have been tricked!" cried Christian. "Are we to die here now, so close to the end?"

Just then another man came up to them. He, too, wore a white robe. But His robe shone like the sun, and His face was fair. In His hand was a whip.

"Did the shepherds not warn you of the false one?" He asked. "The one that led you here disguised himself as an angel of light to deceive you. And did the shepherds not give you a note for your instruction? Why did you not read it when you came to the two roads?"

The shining one then slashed the net with His whip. It broke like a spider's web. And the two friends were free.

"Now I must punish you for following the deceiver," said the shining one. "This will help you remember to follow the instructions you are given on your journey."

He gave each of the men a lash across the back with His whip. "Remember," He said, "I must sometimes punish those whom I love."

Then he led them out of those woods and showed them their road.

Though their backs stung from the whip, Christian and Hopeful felt such love for this being that they wept. "Thank You for Your kindness in rescuing us, Lord," said Christian.

The shining one smiled at them. "Go now," He said. "And beware of evil counsel."

They started up the road. As they went, they sang songs of praises to the Lord.

After they had gone some distance, Christian pointed

ahead on the road. "Look," he said. "Who could this be, who is coming away from Zion?"

"Let us be careful of him!" said Hopeful. "Remember that false one."

When the man reached them he greeted them. "My name is Atheist," he said. "Where are you going?"

"To Mount Zion," said Christian.

At this, the man laughed in scorn. "To Mount Zion!" he said. "In all the world there is no such place. I once sought this city as you do now. I tell you, I have been seeking for twenty years. Twenty years I have wasted!"

"We have heard of and we believe in such a place," said Christian.

"Then look for it, Fool!" laughed Atheist. "You will never find it."

"The Lord Himself put us on this path," said Christian. "For we walk by faith, not by sight."*

They turned away from the man named Atheist. He stood laughing at them as they walked away.

Soon the road passed through a wide field full of flowers. As far as the men could see, there was nothing but flowers. They walked on and on. Their going became slower and slower. Their feet seemed to grow heavy. Hopeful yawned.

"Christian," he said. "I am so tired I can hardly hold my eyes open. Let us take some sleep here." He sank to the ground.

---

*2 Corinthians 5:7

"No!" said Christian. "If we fall asleep here, we may never wake up!"

"What do you mean?" asked Hopeful, startled.

"Remember the shepherds' warning against the Enchanted Ground. This must be the place," said Christian. "This sleepiness is not natural. We must stay awake!" He helped Hopeful up.

"Let us talk to each other, to stay awake," said Christian. "Tell me how you came to have faith."

So Hopeful said, "In the town of Vanity, I lived like those others you saw at the fair. I loved the treasures of the world. As I bought them, I wanted them more and more. And I lived an evil life.

"But when you and Faithful came there, you appeared clean, where everyone else seemed filthy. And I heard Faithful say he bought only the truth. Then shame and sorrow began growing in my soul. I began to pray and to weep. But daily I grew worse. The things I once loved, I now hated. I hated even myself.

"Then Faithful said to me, 'Just believe in Jesus Christ, and He will set you free.' So I cried out to Him to forgive me. Then I wept, first in sorrow, and then in joy."

As the two men talked of these things, their weariness washed away. And so they passed safely through the Enchanted Ground.

Chapter 10

The two men had not gone far when they noticed a man behind them. They called to him, but he seemed not to hear. He came on slowly.

The men greeted him and asked him about himself.

"My name is Ignorance," the man said. "I come from a land called Conceit. I am going to the Celestial City."

"Then join us, Friend," said Hopeful.

"I would rather walk alone," said Ignorance. "I will get to the city in my own time."

"How far have you journeyed?" asked Christian.

"Not far," the other said. "My country is near the Delectable Mountains. I got on this road there."

"So you did not come in at the gate?"

"The gate!" Everyone knows that is a long way off. No, no. Why should I travel that far, just to return the same way?"

Christian and Hopeful looked at each other gravely.

Then Christian said to Ignorance, "But because you were not invited in at the wicket gate, you were not given anything to show at the gates to the city. Without some token to show that you are a guest here, you cannot be invited in."

"I think I can," said Ignorance. "I have lived a good life. I pray. I give money to the poor. The Lord will accept me for these things."

"You cannot gain entrance by the things you do," said

Christian. "Your own righteousness (goodness and purity) will count for nothing at the gate. Only those who are made righteous by believing in the Son of God can enter."

"I know I am righteous," said Ignorance. "My own heart tells me so."

Christian said, "A wise man said, 'He that trusteth in his own heart is a fool.' "*

"That was spoken of an evil heart," said Ignorance. "Mine is good."

"How do you know your heart is good?" asked Christian.

"Because it comforts me with hopes of heaven," said Ignorance.

"Your heart can deceive you. You may hope for things and yet have no reason for hope, because without Christ in your heart, you have no promise," said Christian.

"But isn't a good heart one that has good thoughts?" asked Ignorance. "And isn't a good life one that is in obedience to God's commandments?"

"Yes, indeed," said Christian. "But it is one thing to have goodness, and another just to think you do."

"Why, what do you mean?" asked Ignorance.

"Your thoughts must agree with the Word of God," said Christian. "If they do not, they are not God's thoughts. And the Word of God says, 'There is none righteous, no, not one.'† So if your thoughts tell you that you are righteous, as you say,

---

*Proverbs 28:26

†Romans 3:10

then your thoughts are not from God."

Ignorance seemed confused. "Then, what would my thoughts be if they were from God?" he asked.

"Your thoughts would condemn you," said Christian, "because they would tell you the truth about yourself. And the truth is that, apart from Christ, you live in evil. As His Word says, 'Every imagination of the thoughts of his heart was only evil continually.'*

"Now, when your heart tells you that you are good, you are blinded to the truth about yourself," continued Christian. "And in that condition, you cannot enter the City of God."

"But you say I must believe in Christ," said Ignorance. "I do believe in Him."

"What do you believe of Him?" asked Christian.

"That He died for everyone, and that He now accepts us if we obey Him," said Ignorance.

"This belief of yours is not found in the Word of God," said Christian.

Ignorance grew angry. "What do you mean?" he said.

Christian explained. "This faith is not in Christ," he said, "but in yourself. True faith does not come from yourself, but from God Himself. We cannot believe in Jesus as we wish to, but only as He really is. And He makes us acceptable to God by His own obedience, not by ours. He obeyed God His Father and died on the cross. Now, no one can come to God except through Christ. And only God can reveal Christ in a person's heart."

---

*Genesis 6:5

"Ignorance," he said, "if you ask God to show you His son Christ, He will. And Christ will show you your heart as it really is. And when He shows you the evil that lives in your heart, ask for His forgiveness, and He will give you a new heart. Then you can enter His city."

CHAPTER 11

Christian and Hopeful now walked alone. Ignorance still would not go with them.

"You have your belief, and I have mine," he said. "You go on your way. I will come along as I wish." And he waited behind until they were out of sight.

"I pity this poor man," Christian said to Hopeful as they walked. "He will come all the way to the gates in his ignorance and not enter."

Soon Christian and Hopeful noticed that the land was changing. It was no longer harsh and desolate. Here were flowers and meadows and trees and birds. As the men walked they saw these things more and more. The sun, too, grew brighter and brighter.

Now they came to fruit trees, gardens, and vineyards. Here and there were openings in the wall by the road. These openings led into the gardens and orchards. In one of these gardens stood a gardener.

"Hello," he said. "Welcome to Beulah Land."

"These gardens are the King's," said the gardener. "They are for His delight and for any pilgrims who come here. Rest here if you wish."

Christian and Hopeful walked among the fruit trees and gardens, delighting in the beauty of the place. They found a vineyard of fat, juicy grapes, sweeter than any they had ever tasted. After eating their fill, they lay down and slept.

When they woke they felt fresh and strong. Just as they began to go on, two men in clothes that shone like pure gold met them.

"We have come to bring you to the city," the men said. "You are at the end of your journey. But before you can enter, you must face one more test."

"Will you go with us to help us?" asked Christian.

"We will go with you," they said. "But you must win through this test by your faith."

Now they all went on together until they came within sight of the city.

It was made of gold and precious jewels. It was so bright that Christian and Hopeful could not stare at it long. There, in front of the city, were two massive gates made of a single pearl.

But before the castle on the mountain was a deep, wide river. There was no bridge.

"How do we get across?" said Christian.

"By your faith," said one of the men. "You will find the water as deep or as shallow as your faith is."

Christian went first. He took a few steps, then suddenly sank in up to his chin. "Help me!" he cried. "The water is going over my head!"

Hopeful stepped into the water. "Courage, Christian!" he said. "See?" I stand on the bottom. You can, too."

But Christian floundered in the water. Hopeful reached out to him.

Hopeful struggled to keep his friend's head out of the water.

"I am being punished for my sins," gasped Christian. "The Lord wishes to drown me here, so I will not enter His city."

"Christian!" said Hopeful. "This is not punishment! It is the test the shining one spoke of."

Suddenly Christian remembered. The test! "Give me faith, Lord!" he cried. Then suddenly his feet found the bottom.

Soon he and Hopeful stood on the other side of the river.

Then the two friends started up the long hill toward the city. As they went, crowds of people came down, laughing, singing, and dancing, to meet them and walk with them. Now Christian and Hopeful sang, too.

And all the people and all their praises went up the holy mountain into the clouds and into the City of Heaven.

THE PILGRIM'S PROGRESS

PART TWO

CHAPTER 1

In the City of Destruction there was great talk. The people there had heard rumors and reports of Christian's journey to the Celestial City. They heard of his battle with the winged terror, Apollyon, of his being captured by the giant Despair, and of his going through the Valley of the Shadow of Death.

And, last, they heard of his entering the City of Heaven. Some in the City of Destruction still called Christian a fool. But many more now called him a hero. A few secretly wished that they, too, were brave enough to go on such a pilgrimage.

Christian's wife, Christiana, grew more and more troubled. She missed her husband so! And she remembered how terribly she had treated him in his anguish. His cry, "What must I do to be saved?" still rang in her ears. He had begged her to go with him. And she had scorned him!

One day Christiana burst into tears. "Oh, why did I not believe him?" she cried. "I could have gone with him. Because I sinned, he is gone from us forever!"

Her four sons heard her, and they wept, too.

That night Christiana had a dream. First, she dreamed a roll of paper came down from heaven and opened to her. In it was written every bad thing she had done in her life. She cried out, "Lord, forgive me! I have sinned!"

Then she dreamed that two evil-looking men stood by her bed. "What shall we do with her?" one said. "If she goes on like this, we will lose her just as we lost her husband." The other hissed through his teeth, like a snake.

Christiana woke in a cold sweat. She got on her knees and prayed. Then she woke her sons. "Come!" she said. "We must leave."

Soon a knock came at the door. A man entered.

"Peace to this house," he said. "I am Secret. I live with those in the house of the Lord. I have been sent to give you this." He handed her a letter written in letters of gold. "It is the King's invitation to His palace," said Secret. "Keep it with you. You must give it at the gates of the city when you come there. Your journey begins at the wicket gate, as did your husband's."

Then there was great excitement in Christiana's house. Quickly she and her sons prepared to leave.

Later that day, two neighbors, Mrs. Timorous and Mercy, stopped to visit.

"Where are you off to?" asked Mrs. Timorous.

"We are going to where my husband, Christian, has gone," said Christiana.

"Oh, what madness!" said Mrs. Timorous. "First your husband and now you!"

But Mercy was silent.

Christiana told her visitors of her dream and of her special visitor. She showed them her invitation from the King.

Mrs. Timorous only sneered. "Come, Mercy," she said. "Let us leave fools to themselves. We have better things to do than to visit with the likes of her."

But Mercy stood still. "I think I will go a little way with Christiana," she said. "I wish to see her off on her journey."

"I see you are taken with silliness, too," snapped Mrs. Timorous. "Well, let fools go where they will, I always say." She hurried away.

Then Christiana, her four sons, and Mercy set out across the fields toward the wicket gate. Christiana was glad for Mercy's company. The two talked in the warm sunshine as they went.

Mrs. Timorous scurried around to all her friends' houses to spread this last bit of gossip. "Oh!" she said. "You will never guess what has just happened."

CHAPTER 2

As the two women walked, Mercy seemed to grow troubled.

"What is wrong?" asked Christiana.

"My heart is sad," said Mercy. "Soon I must leave you and go back. I wish I would never have to see that city again."

"Then come with us!" said Christiana. "I would dearly love to have your company."

"But I cannot," said Mercy. She began to weep. "You have an invitation from the King. He has not invited me. Perhaps I am not wanted there."

"You may come at my invitation. I do not believe the King would turn away anyone who desires to come to Him."

"But I do not have the hope that you do."

"Go at least to the wicket gate with us," said Christiana. "It will not take us long to get there. And when we come to the gate, I will plead with the gatekeeper for you." And Mercy agreed to this.

As they walked, Christiana suddenly said, "Stop!"

Just ahead lay the swampy ground where her husband had fallen, the Slough of Despond. Pliable, who had also fallen in with Christian, had told all the town of that place.

"Look," said Mercy. "There are steps through it. Let us go carefully."

One after another, they made it across. The rest of the day went well. They met no trouble; they were at the wicket gate.

Christiana knocked. There was no answer. She knocked again, harder. Still no answer. They stood wondering what to do, when suddenly behind them came the barking of what sounded like a giant dog. Terrified, Christiana knocked again, harder and harder.

"Who is there?" came a voice. At the sound of the voice, the barking stopped.

"I am Christiana," she said. "We have come to take the road my husband traveled. May we enter?"

The gate opened. "Come in, wife of Christian," said the keeper. "And you," He said to the boys, "you children are always welcome here."

Christiana and the boys went in. The gate shut. And Mercy was left outside!

"Oh!" she cried. "I cannot enter! Now I will be torn to pieces by that dog!" And she fainted.

Inside, Christiana said, "My Lord, I have a friend outside who wishes to go with me to the City of the King. She fears she can not come in here because she was not invited."

The keeper opened the gate and saw Mercy lying on the ground. Quickly He took her hand and helped her up.

"Oh, Lord," she said. "I was not invited. But I ask You to have pity on me, too, and to let me in."

"I give life to all who believe in Me," He said, smiling. And He led her in through the gate.

Then the keeper asked Christiana, "Why did you knock so hard?"

"We were afraid to be left outside," she said. "And I

believed that our only hope was to get in through the gate."

"Your faith has opened this door," said the keeper. "That dog you heard was sent by an evil one to frighten away pilgrims. Many have heard him bark and have fled this gate."

Then the keeper showed them their road, and they started out.

They had not gone far when two men jumped over the wall by the roadside. Christiana gasped! They were the men she had seen in her dream.

Just as they were about to grab her, a voice said, "Stop!" They turned and ran.

The voice belonged to a tall soldier. "I am of the house of the keeper," he said. "Do not fear. Soon the Lord will send a guide to protect you on your journey."

CHAPTER 3

Christiana, her sons, and Mercy next came to the same place where Christian had stopped, the house of the Interpreter. Here they knocked and were invited in.

"We of this house are very glad you have come, Christiana," said the Interpreter. "We have already heard of your starting on this journey. The Lord's messengers travel fast. Now, come. While our dinner is being prepared, let me show you some things."

And he took them into the same rooms he had showed Christian and explained everything to them. Then he took them to some other rooms.

In the first of these, a man was raking a pile of straw and dirt. Before him stood another man who held out a crown. But the raker would not take the crown.

"The riches of the world are like straw and dirt," said the Interpreter. "This man would rather have them than an eternal crown."

Then the Interpreter took them into the best room in the house. It was very beautiful. But on one wall sat a poisonous spider.

"Tell me what you see here," said the Interpreter.

They all looked around the room.

"I see nothing special," said Mercy.

"Look again," he said.

"I see a spider on the wall," she said.

"Is there just one spider here?" he asked.

Christiana began to weep. "Sir," she said, "there are two. And one of the spiders is much more poisonous than the other. I was like a poisonous spider when I scorned my husband for his faith. With my sharp tongue, my bite was more deadly than that spider's."

The Interpreter smiled. "And yet," he said, "like this spider, the person who is full of the poison of sin may yet come to repent and live in the very best room in the King's palace."

Now the Interpreter led the group outside and into his garden. There on the grass hopped a little robin. In its mouth was a great black spider.

"This robin is like many people who pretend to be Christians," said the Interpreter. "They, like this robin, are nice to look at and are thought well of by other people. In the streets and the churches they appear blameless. But at home, when no one is watching, they greedily gobble down sin like poison."

Soon dinner was ready. A table laden with all kinds of meats, fruits, and pastries was set up in the garden under the branches of sweet smelling lilac trees. The Interpreter called his minstrels, and they came and played and sang and danced.

Christiana, her sons, Mercy, and all the people of the house ate and talked and laughed together under the stars, long into the night.

Christiana and Mercy woke with the sun the next morning. They went out into the garden, where they met a lady of the house.

"A bath has been prepared for you," said the lady. "Before you leave, you must first wash from yourselves the soil of that country beyond the wicket gate."

After they had bathed, they were brought new, white linen gowns. The boys, too, were bathed and given new clothes.

Then the Interpreter came into the garden. He lightly drew a mark on the two women's foreheads.

"This is the King's mark," he said. "Now you will be known as His wherever you are."

Now the Interpreter called, and out of the house came a tall, strong man. At his side hung a great sword. On his bearded face were many faded battle scars.

"I am Great-heart," he said, bowing low. "I will take you to the House Beautiful."

With Great-heart leading them, the group now set out on the narrow road. Soon they came to the cross on the hill, where Christian's burden had fallen off.

Here they stopped. They all stared at the cross. As they stood there, tears came to their eyes. Everyone knelt and worshipped.

"The one Who died here carried our sins on His own shoulders," said Great-heart. "He obeyed God and came here to be punished for us. And with His blood He washes us clean, we who will believe in Him. It is by His death that you are able to go on this journey to His city."

"So it was this that made Christian's burden fall off here!" said Christiana. "Now that I am here I, too, feel as though a great weight has lifted off me."

"No one ever need carry his burden past this cross," said Great-heart.

After they had worshipped a little longer, they started out again. The road went down the hill from the cross and then started to climb again.

Just before this hill, by the side of the road, three men hung from their arms and legs in iron collars. They stared in misery at the pilgrims.

"Who are these men, and why do they hang here?" asked Mercy.

"Their names are Simple, Sloth, and Presumption," said Great-heart. "For years they have lain here by the road and called out to pilgrims as they passed. 'Leave the road,' they would say, 'and eat and drink with us. Enjoy yourselves. There is no need for you to walk this hard road.'

"They said many evil things about the Lord, as well," continued Great-heart. "With their lies, they have turned away many pilgrims on this road. These men hang here now in punishment for their wicked deeds."

Just a little past the three men, at the bottom of the hill, ran a stream. The travelers were thirsty and went to the stream for a drink. But the water was too muddy to drink.

"This stream is where Christian quenched his thirst before climbing the Hill of Difficulty here," said Great-heart. "It was once clean and good. But evil beings have come in over the wall to tramp in the waters and muddy it with their feet. They do this simply because they hate all pilgrims to the Celestial City."

"Can we do nothing to quench our thirst?" asked Christiana.

"Yes," said Great-heart. "Put some water in a clean vessel. The mud will settle to the bottom, and the water will be clean again."

So they did this. After a little while, when the mud had settled, they all drank some water. Refreshed, they started up the long climb.

At the top of the hill, Great-heart told the group of the lions ahead. "But do not fear them," he said. "They are chained."

And soon they came to the lions. But the lions were not alone. Behind them on the road stood a giant. His huge arms were smeared with dried, blackened blood.

"If you come any farther, I will kill you!" he roared.

Everyone stared in horror. Everyone except Great-heart. Out flashed his great sword.

"You stand in the King's highway!" he thundered. "I am the King's champion. Your days of murdering pilgrims are over!"

The giant roared in laughter.

But the laughter soon died in his throat. Never had he faced such a foe!

Great-heart came on. His sword blade a flash of whistling fury, he chopped at the giant. Again and again and again.

Finally, like an oak tree crashing to the ground, down came the giant.

Great-heart led the frightened pilgrims past the lions. The lions roared and lurched against their chains. Christiana and Mercy shuddered as they walked past the dead giant.

Soon it would be dark. Ahead lay the House Beautiful. "We must hurry," said Great-heart. "It is not good to be out here after dark."

When they came to the house, Great-heart called out. The porter inside knew Great-heart's voice because the warrior had many times led pilgrims this way.

"Come in," said the porter. "Welcome."

"This is Christiana," said Great-heart, "the wife of Christian, who stayed here before. She and her people here are going to the Celestial City." Great-heart turned to go.

"What!" cried Christiana. "Please do not leave us!"

"I must return tonight," he said. "You did not ask my Lord for a guide, so He cannot send me farther. Yet, you may still ask Him this, and I will return."

"Christiana, wife of Christian," said the porter, "we have been expecting you. Your husband stayed here on his journey. You are among friends here. Now, come. Dinner is waiting."

They all sat down to a delicious meal of roast lamb. They ate and ate. Then the pilgrims were shown to their sleeping rooms.

Mercy and Christiana shared a room. They lay awake a

little while, talking excitedly about their journey. From somewhere in the house came soft music that fell on their ears like raindrops of joy.

In the morning Christiana said, "Mercy, why were you laughing last night?"

"I must have laughed in my dream," said Mercy. "I dreamed I was alone in darkness, and voices were laughing at me. I was weeping. Then a bright being came, wiped my tears, and led me to a golden palace. Inside sat the King on His throne. 'Welcome, Daughter,' He said."

Christiana and Mercy went downstairs to breakfast. Three girls of the house, Prudence, Piety, and Charity, ate with them.

"Please stay here with us for as long as you like," said Prudence. "We love having you here."

So they stayed there for many days. They grew to love the people of the house. They spent their time walking about the grounds outside or sitting indoors, talking and laughing with one another. Christiana, Mercy, and the boys learned much of the wisdom of God from Prudence, Piety, and Charity.

One night, Mercy and Christiana lay awake talking. A soothing breeze danced in through their open window. Mercy stared out at the stars glittering in the summer sky.

"I love this house," she said dreamily. "I wish we could stay here forever."

"The Lord is so good to us," said Christiana. "Just think! Someday I will see my dear husband again in paradise."

One day Christiana's oldest son, Matthew, became very ill.

"Call Mr. Skill," said Prudence.

"Who is this Mr. Skill?" asked Christiana.

"He is the good doctor," said Prudence, "one of the King's subjects. He has helped people for as long as anyone can remember. No one knows how old he is."

Soon the doctor came and examined Matthew. "Something poisonous lies within," he said. "What has he eaten?"

"Nothing but the good food of this house," said Christiana.

"Wait," said another son, Samuel. "Just inside the wicket gate, an apple tree hung over the wall onto the road. Matthew ate an apple."

"Ah," said the doctor. "That tree belongs to the evil Beelzebub. It hangs over the wall to tempt pilgrims. Its fruit is deadly."

He gave Matthew a drink of something. Matthew fell asleep.

"This medicine will cleanse your son as he sleeps," said Mr. Skill.

The doctor made some of this medicine into pills. He gave them to Christiana to take along on their journey.

"This is mixed with tears of repentance," he said. "It will cure any disease that pilgrims may fall into."

Soon the day came when the travelers began preparing to leave.

Then Christiana remembered. Great-heart! They could not go without him. Quickly she wrote a letter asking the Interpreter to send his guide. The porter of House Beautiful sent a messenger with the letter.

A few days later Great-heart arrived. "My Lord, the

Interpreter, sends each of you this bread," he said to Christiana and Mercy. "And to you boys, these figs and raisins. These will refresh you on your journey."

Prudence, Piety, Charity, and the porter all walked with the travelers down the road. Everyone embraced and said good-bye. Then the pilgrims set out.

The road down into the Valley of Humiliation was very steep. Everyone went down carefully. At the bottom, the land opened out into softly rolling hills.

"We need not be afraid of this valley," said Great-heart. "Here the humble may walk in peace. Only those who think highly of themselves find danger here. The Word says, 'God resisteth the proud, but giveth grace unto the humble.' "*

The travelers did not hurry here. They walked through green meadows and fields of lilies. Butterflies flitted about, and the songs of birds filled the air.

"Our Lord used to love to come here," said Great-heart. "He loved to walk these meadows and breathe this sweet air. And here men have met angels and found pearls. There is none of the noise and troubles and confusions of life here. Only peace and beauty. No one walks here but those who love to walk a pilgrim's life."

Soon they came to a small, flat, grassy plain.

"This place is called Forgetful Green," said Great-heart. "Here is where Christian had his battle with the winged beast, Apollyon. There is still some of Christian's blood that can be seen on the stones here. And a few broken darts from Apollyon still lie shattered in the grass.

---

*James 4:6

"Your father fought a great battle here," he said to the boys. "Hercules himself could have done no better against Apollyon. Come, let me show you something."

Great-heart led the group a little past the plain. There stood a stone monument. Great-heart read the words carved on it:

"Here was a battle fought, most strange and yet most true. Christian and Apollyon sought each other to subdue. The man so bravely played the man, he made the fiend to fly. Of which a monument I stand, the same to testify."

After this, the road went down again. The land became rock-strewn and barren. There was no sound of birds.

"We are coming to the Valley of the Shadow of Death," said Great-heart, "Follow right behind me and stay close together."

As they went forward they began to hear voices in the air. The voices were moaning and screaming. They grew louder and louder. The women's faces were pale. The boys were shivering.

"Have courage!" said Great-heart. "But watch your steps carefully. There are snares here."

Suddenly the ground began moving under their feet.

"Quickly!" shouted Great-heart. They leaped forward. The ground collapsed behind them.

Then began a hissing in the air, like a great serpent.

Christiana gasped. "Look!" she screamed. "Something is coming toward us on the road. I have never seen such a shape!"

"Stay behind me!" said Great-heart. He whipped out his

sword. "I will meet this fiend."

Great-heart strode down the path toward the thing. It kept coming. Closer and closer. Now it was towering over Great-heart. But he never stopped.

Then the thing spread out two vast wings. Great-heart raised his sword.

And the thing vanished!

Great-heart came back to the group. "You see?" he said. " 'Resist the devil, and he will flee from you.'* Let us go forward."

"Thank the Lord for such a brave guide!" said Christiana.

Suddenly Mercy screamed. "Behind us!" she cried. "A great lion is stalking us!"

A deafening roar shook the ground.

Great-heart took to the rear of the group. The lion charged! And Great-heart went to meet it head-on.

Now the lion slowed its charge, then stopped. Great-heart kept going!

Suddenly the lion turned and loped off down the path.

Great-heart took his place in front again and led the group onward. "Just a little farther," he said.

They had not gone far when suddenly a black mist settled over them. They were covered in inky darkness.

"Do not fear!" said Great-heart. "Stand still, everyone. We will win through this, too."

Suddenly the hairs on the back of Christiana's neck stood

---

*James 4:7

on end. She opened her mouth to scream, but no sound came out. From out of the writhing mist, a cold hand had touched her face!

Now she and the rest of the group heard and felt the air moving around them. Things flitted past them in the darkness. Hollow voices moaned and howled among them.

Then Great-heart's voice boomed out, "Lord, let your light shine on our darkness!"

And light came.

Like lightning from heaven, it flashed to the earth. It split the darkness with a crackle.

And in that light that was brighter than sunlight, the travelers went on through the valley.

The travelers were almost out of the valley when they came to a cave by the road.

"Great-heart!" came a huge voice from inside the cave.

Everyone stopped. Out of the cave stepped a giant. His name was Maul. "Great-heart," he said. "This is your last journey! You have robbed the prince of this world of too many people. And this group with you will never see the city of light."

"I am the King's servant," said Great-heart. "He has commanded me to guide His people from the darkness to the light. Do not oppose me! I come against you with the strength of the Lord."

The giant lumbered toward Great-heart swinging a massive club. Great-heart drew his sword.

But this giant was quick! His club smashed down onto

Great-heart's head. Great-heart dropped to his knees.

The travelers gasped. "Great-heart!" screamed Mercy.

The giant's club came whistling down again.

Just as the club came down, Great-heart rolled to the side. He drove up, slashing at the giant's arm.

The giant staggered back, his arm bleeding. He howled in fury.

The two fought for more than an hour. The giant was panting so hard that steam blew out of his nostrils. "Hold!" he gasped. "Let us rest."

Great-heart agreed. As the giant lay down to catch his breath, Great-heart came back to the group. He was breathing hard. Blood was running down his face. He knelt and prayed for strength.

The giant was rested. "Now you die!" he said, swinging his club.

But Great-heart, ducking a savage blow, drove his blade clear through the giant. As the giant sank to his knees, Great-heart swiped off his head.

Then everyone shouted and laughed and clapped one another on the back.

CHAPTER 7

It was growing dark when the band of pilgrims came out of the valley. As the road climbed, the land grew friendlier. Here and there were trees, and here grass grew again.

They came to an old man sleeping under a tall oak tree. They knew he was a pilgrim by his clothes and his staff.

Gently, Great-heart woke him. "You should not be lying out here when darkness comes," he said.

"I must have fallen asleep," the man said. "I was so tired, I lay down here. I have come on a hard journey."

"Come with us," said Great-heart. "These are pilgrims, too. We would welcome your company.

"This is Christiana," said Great-heart, "the wife of Christian, who came this way before. These are her sons, and this is her friend."

The man's eyes went wide. "Christian's wife!" he said. "Christian's name is spoken all through these parts!

"My name is Honest," the man continued. "I would be honored to join your company."

They set out together. They walked for hours in the darkness. The women and the boys grew weary.

"Just ahead is an inn," said Honest. "The owner is a good man. His name is Gaius. I know him well. He will let us stay with him tonight."

When they got to the inn, all was dark. Honest knocked.

Soon a lantern shone in the window. "Who is there?" came a voice from inside.

"It is your friend, Honest," he said. "My friends and I need a place to sleep tonight.

They were welcomed inside and given rooms. The exhausted pilgrims immediately fell asleep.

But Great-heart and old Honest sat up with Gaius all through the night, sharing what news they had and talking of the kingdom of heaven.

At breakfast the next morning Gaius said, "Mr. Great-heart, I have heard much of your great strength and fierceness in battle. You are truly the King's champion.

"There is one thing I wish to ask you," continued Gaius. "Not far from here lives a giant. He is called Slay-good. He has killed many of the Lord's pilgrims. No one can come against him. We of this land would be forever grateful if you could rid us of him."

"Take me to him!" said Great-heart. He buckled on his sword.

Gaius brought Great-heart to the giant's cave. The giant clutched a man in his fist. The man whimpered as the giant poked at him, feeling his ribs.

"Giant!" said Great-heart. "Now you will pay for murdering the King's subjects!"

The giant dropped the man and reached out with long arms to crush this new enemy. But soon the giant lay dead on the ground.

Now Great-heart went up to the man he had saved from

the giant. "Who are you, and how did this giant capture you?" he asked.

"My name is Feeble-mind," said the man. He was pale and very skinny. "I have been very sick. I decided to go to the Celestial City. Weak that I am, I thought that if I could not run, I could walk, and if I could not walk, I could crawl. But as I was going, this giant caught me. He was trying to fatten me up before he ate me."

"Come to my inn," said Gaius. "I welcome all pilgrims. Stay as long as you like."

So Feeble-mind went with them.

Soon after, a man on crutches came to the inn. He, too, was a pilgrim. But his journey was a long one because of his crutches. He and Feeble-mind became good friends over the days that followed.

After many days had passed, the pilgrims set out. They said good-bye to Gaius, thanking him for his kindness.

But Feeble-mind hung back. "You go ahead of me," he said. "I cannot go as quickly as you, and I do not wish to be a burden to you."

"My brother," said Great-heart, "my duty is to comfort the feeble-minded and to support the weak. I will not leave you behind."

The crippled man, Mr. Ready-to-halt, came up to Feeble-mind. "Take one of my crutches if you wish," he said. "I do not need both, and we can go together, you and I, at our own pace."

So they started. Their way took them through the town

of Vanity, where Faithful had been killed. But they passed through safely. Because of Faithful's death, many in that town now believed in the kingdom of God.

The pilgrims then came to the River of God. Here they rested, eating fruit from the orchards and lying in the soft meadows before setting out again.

Now as they went on, they came to a meadow on one side of the road. Through the meadow ran a path that went alongside the road. Here Great-heart stopped.

"Doubting Castle lies beyond that meadow," he said. "That is where Giant Despair lives."

On hearing the name, Christiana gasped. She had heard of her husband's trouble with that giant.

"It is time to end the reign of Despair," said Great-heart. "I have come this way for many years, but now I must deal with this evil giant. My Lord has bid me destroy both Despair and Doubt."

"Let me go with you, Great-heart," said old Honest. "I have fought many a battle in my day. I can still wield a sword against wickedness."

Great-heart left Feeble-mind and Ready-to-halt to guard the women and children in the road. Then he and Honest went to the castle.

Great-heart strode to the doors of the courtyard and called to the giant.

"Who calls me?" roared Despair.

"It is I," said Great-heart, "the King's champion. I have

come to destroy you and your castle! You will never again rob the Lord of His people!"

The heavy doors flew open. "I have come against angels!" said the giant. "Who are you to challenge me?" And he came out bellowing and swinging his club.

Great-heart and Honest had never fought so hard in their lives! The giant swung his heavy club with terrible strength. As the two men dodged his blows, the giant's club pounded deep into the earth, spewing out dirt and stones.

Suddenly, from out of the castle came another giant, howling and cursing!

This was Despair's wife, Diffidence. She came at the two men with a great, curve-bladed knife.

Quickly, old Honest met her charge. He ducked as she swung her knife. Then, with all his strength he lashed out, cutting her almost in two. Down she tumbled.

Now Honest turned to help his friend. Coming from behind, he hacked at the giant's legs. Howling, the giant fell to his knees.

Now Great-heart saw his chance. He leaped in and struck with the force of thunder. His sword came down on the giant's head, shattering his steel cap like glass.

Both giants lay dead.

The two men were panting and bleeding from their battle. They lay down to rest. Great-heart said, "Now we must tear this castle down to the ground. Despair and Doubt will never again turn pilgrims out of the way."

It took seven days to destroy Doubting Castle. Swinging

great iron clubs, Great-heart and Honest smashed stones and splintered wooden beams. Whole walls crumbled. Tall towers fell.

In one courtyard were piles and piles of men's bones. These were all of the pilgrims the giant had killed.

In the dungeons, Great-heart found a man and a girl chained to a wall. They were starved almost to death. Great-heart broke their chains.

"I am Despondency," said the man. "This is my daughter, Much-afraid. We cannot ever thank you enough, great one!"

"Come with us," said Great-heart.

When Christiana and the others saw Great-heart and Honest coming, they all began laughing and shouting. Then there was singing and dancing in the road! Even Ready-to-halt danced, hobbling about on just one crutch.

Mr. Despondency and his daughter were given food and drink. They wept for joy as they ate, and strength and life came into them again.

Now that Despair and Doubt were gone, the pilgrims went more easily up the road. Even Feeble-mind felt stronger. And Ready-to-halt walked more steadily, his crutch only lightly touching the ground.

They came this way into the Delectable Mountains.

"Welcome, Mr. Great-heart, and all of your friends," said the shepherds of these mountains. "The feeble and the weak, as well as the strong and the mighty, are always welcome here."

So the travelers rested here. Over the days that followed,

they were shown the things that were shown Christian and Hopeful before. And the shepherds showed them some new things.

They climbed a mountain called Innocent. There they saw a man in white clothes. Two other men, Prejudice and Ill-will, were throwing dirt on the man in white. But the dirt would just fall off, and the man's clothes were as white as ever.

"Who is this man?" asked Christiana.

One of the shepherds said, "This man is named Godlyman. His white garment shows that his life is innocent of all evil. The other two here are evil. They hate those who are innocent. But God Himself clothes the innocent, and He does not allow the dirt of sin to soil them."

Then they climbed another mountain called Charity. There, a man sat cutting clothes from a bundle of cloth. Piles of these clothes lay all around him. Yet for all he cut, he did not run out of cloth.

"This man makes clothes for the poor," said a shepherd. "This is to show you that whoever gives to the poor will always have enough for himself."

The pilgrims stayed with the shepherds for several days. When it came time to leave, the shepherds said, "The way from here has many dangers. But they cannot conquer you, because your guide is Great-heart."

The road from the mountains went down through a thick forest. The pilgrims had not gone far when they came upon a man with a sword in his hand. He was tall and sinewy. Blood ran down his face and arms and down his hand onto his sword blade.

Great-heart gripped his sword. "Who are you?" he called.

The man was breathing hard. "I am called Valiant-for-truth," he said. "I am a pilgrim to the holy city. As I came this way, three men stopped me on the road. They said their names were Wild-head, Inconsiderate, and Pragmatic. They told me I was to choose to join them, to turn back, or to die."

"And you chose to fight?" said Great-heart.

"I did. We fought for hours. They just now ran off as they heard you coming. Though I bleed from their wounds, they bleed from many more that I gave them."

Great-heart was beaming, "Now here is a fighting man!" he said. "Three against one!"

"Those odds are nothing to a man who has the truth on his side," said Valiant-for-truth. "As it is written, 'Though an host should encamp against me, my heart shall not fear.' "*

"You have done well!" said Great-heart. "You have resisted unto blood, fighting against evil. Now, come. Let us wash your wounds."

When this was done, and they went on, Great-heart walked with Valiant-for-truth.

"Where are you from?" asked Great-heart.

"A place called Dark Land," said the other.

"Dark Land! That is an evil place. How did you come to leave there and travel this road?"

"One day, a man named Tell-true came into my land and

---

*Psalm 27:3

told us of a man named Christian who fought his way to the holy city. On hearing this, a burning desire grew in my heart to do the same."

Then Great-heart said to Christiana, "You see? The story of your husband's faith has traveled all over this land."

"What!" said Valiant-for-truth, turning to Christiana. "You are Christian's wife?"

"Yes," she said. "And my sons and I have turned from unbelief to belief and now travel to the city, too."

"That day will be glad," said Valiant-for-truth, "when Christian's family comes to him in the city."

"Tell me," said Great-heart, "are you the only one from your land to come on this journey?"

"Yes," said Valiant-for-truth. "All the others, even my own family, reminded me of all the dangers. They told of Giant Despair, of Apollyon, of the Valley of Death, and the rest. For fear of those things, no one would go with me. But I believed in the truth of Mr. Tell-true's story. And I believed that by faith I could overcome any danger on my journey."

When the travelers came to the place called the Enchanted Ground, Great-heart sent Valiant-for-truth to the rear of the company. "You guard from the rear," he said, "and I, from the front."

Since Christian and Hopeful had passed, this place had grown over with briars and thorns. Only here and there showed the enchanted flowers. Yet it was still a dangerous place. Great-heart and Valiant-for-truth went with their swords drawn.

And danger came quickly. As they walked, suddenly it was dark. A black mist covered them. Now the pilgrims could only follow Great-heart's voice. They held on to one another and groped along. Great-heart ahead, and Valiant-for-truth behind, spoke encouraging words to the other pilgrims. Then everyone began praying aloud to God for deliverance from that evil darkness.

Soon a fresh wind began to blow. The mist began to clear. The wind continued to blow until the darkness had gone.

As the group drew near the end of the Enchanted Ground, they saw a man kneeling by the side of the road. He was praying. Then he got to his feet and started to go on.

"Hello, Friend!" called Great-heart.

The man turned.

"I know this man!" said Honest. "He comes from a

place near my home. His name is Stand-fast." He went up to the stranger.

"Well, Father Honest!" said the man. "Bless me! I did not know you were on this road."

"Indeed!" said Honest. "And these are my friends. Let us go with you."

"Tell us," said Valiant-for-truth. "Why were you praying just now?"

Stand-fast looked grave. "I have just passed through the Enchanted Ground as you have," he said. "It is a terrible place. But its danger does not compare with what I have just now faced. You saw me praying for strength to resist temptation."

"What happened?" asked Honest.

"I had just passed out of the worst of the Enchanted Ground," said Stand-fast. "I was thinking of what a dangerous place that is, where a pilgrim may fall asleep and never wake again. I was thinking I had done well to pass through there, when a lady met me. She was tall and richly dressed. She said, 'Come with me. Be my husband and rule with me. I can give you riches and pleasures you have never dreamed of.'

"Now, I am very poor," continued Stand-fast. "And she was very beautiful. But I told her no. I would stay on the road, I said. She begged me to go with her, but I refused. She would not leave. So I knelt and prayed for deliverance from her. That is when you saw me."

"That lady," said Great-heart, "is a witch! She would have destroyed you.

"Her name is Madam Bubble," continued Great-heart.

"She has been the death of many men who have followed her for her beauty and her wealth. She promises crowns and kingdoms but brings only death and destruction. She leads many to the gallows, many to hell. It is by her sorcery that this land behind us is enchanted."

"And where is she now?" asked Honest.

"After I prayed, I looked up, and she was gone," said Stand-fast. "I do not know where she went."

"She is not far," said Great-heart. "But prayer will keep her away. You are rightly named, my friend, for you stood fast when she came to you."

"Her beauty hides her evil well," said Stand-fast. "Where would she have led me if I had followed her?"

"Only God knows," said Great-heart, grimly. "It was she who led Judas to sell his Lord for thirty pieces of silver."

CHAPTER 10

Now came the end of the journey for the pilgrims.

They came into the King's land, full of beautiful meadows and orchards and vineyards.

The weary pilgrims now stood and stared in wonder at the beauty here. The sun was brighter than they had ever seen, the sky bluer, the grass greener.

And as the travelers stood there, their weariness fell off them like a cloak. Feeble-mind threw his shoulders back like a prince. Ready-to-halt stood up straight and tall and threw away his crutch. The lines and creases were gone from old Honest's face.

Then a sound came to the pilgrims' ears. It was faint at first, as though from far away. It grew and grew.

From over the orchards and gardens, from over the river that lay ahead, from over the mountain past the river, from over the clouds at the top of the mountain—bells were ringing.

Now from out of the clouds on the mountain, down the mountain, across the river, and down the road came a rider on a horse. He flew like the wind.

The rider pulled up to the pilgrims. The horse pranced and blew steam from his nostrils. He was whiter than the whitest linen. On his forehead was a shining silver star.

The rider, too, was clothed in white. His blond hair streamed out over his shoulders. His beard flowed over his broad chest. At his side hung a great sword with a silver handle. He leaped from his horse and bowed to the pilgrims.

"I am the King's messenger," he said. "I have a letter from His Majesty."

He walked up to Christiana and bowed to her. "This is for you," he said.

Christiana's hand trembled as she took the letter. She opened it and read, "Welcome, Christiana, wife of Christian."

"My Lord is calling for me!" cried Christiana. She clapped her hands for joy. "My journey is over. I will see my Lord, the King, and I will see my dear husband again!"

Now down the mountain came horses and chariots and crowds of people, singing and dancing. They stopped at the other side of the river, shouting and calling to Christiana.

The pilgrims went with Christiana up to the river. There she stopped to embrace her friends and to kiss them farewell.

"Do not cry," she said to her sons. "Soon I will see your father again, and you will come, too, when it is your time."

Now she started across the river. She did not stop or sink. She walked across the water. And her friends on this side and all the people on the other side cheered for her.

And she cried, "I am coming, my King!"

Christiana was taken up into the clouds into the city. Now the rest of the pilgrims turned away from the river and walked back down to where they were staying in the gardens.

"The Lord will call each of you in your turn," said Greatheart. "Enjoy yourselves here in His gardens while you wait for Him."

This they did. And they were not alone. There were many gardeners there, tending the King's fruit trees and gardens.

And children came daily to the gardens from the city, to gather flowers and spices for the King's palace. There were never any tears or quarreling among these children, only laughter and singing. Christiana's sons played with the children in the gardens. The heavenly children taught the boys their songs and games.

And when the children wanted to dance, they would come streaming up to Great-heart, and he would play the pipes for them.

The messenger came next for Mr. Ready-to-halt. "The King would like you to dine with Him in His palace," said the messenger.

Ready-to-halt called his friends together. "I am to dine with the King tonight in His palace," he said. "And soon, I know, all of you will be with me there. And thank you, Sir Great-heart, for bringing me safely here. Without you I would have been lost."

And he walked, without his crutches, across the river.

Soon the messenger came for Feeble-mind. "I have come to tell you that your Master wants you," said the messenger. "Now you will see His face in brightness."

Feeble-mind said to his friends, "Now I will leave my feeble mind behind me. I have no need for weakness where I am going."

And as his friends cheered him, he walked boldly across the river shouting, "My faith holds out to the end!"

Now the messenger came back for Mr. Despondency. "Trembling man," said the messenger, "the King summons you. Shout for joy, because He has delivered you from all Doubt."

As Despondency crossed the river he shouted, "Farewell, night! Welcome, day!" His daughter went with him, and they walked up the mountain.

The rest were called for, one by one.

Honest said, "Though I go, I have nothing to leave behind. I take my honesty with me."

"And I," said Valiant-for-truth, "carry my battle scars with me. Yet I leave my sword for any who has the courage and skill to use it."

When the last had gone over, Great-heart stood alone on this side of the river. Now he shouted for joy.

"Hail, Lord!" he cried. "May all Your people praise You forever! Now I return, to bring more pilgrims to You."

And he turned and walked back down the road, tightening his sword-belt.

ROBINSON CRUSOE

MAN ON A DESERT ISLAND

by Daniel Defoe
retold by Dan Larsen

INTRODUCTION

The Life and Strange Surprising Adventures of Robinson Crusoe was first published in 1719. Since then, the name has been shortened to *Robinson Crusoe,* the title most of us know it by. Probably almost everyone has read or at least heard of this title once in life, and for good reason: This book is one of the most widely read pieces of fiction ever written.

This is the story of a young man who runs away from home and seeks adventure and excitement as a seaman aboard a ship. He does indeed find adventure, though much more than he had hoped for. He is shipwrecked on a remote island, where he lives most of his life alone.

This could be the end of the story for Robinson Crusoe, but it's really only the beginning. On the island he begins to wonder about many things. Eventually he makes many discoveries—some strange, some horrible, and some—well, that would give the story away.

CHAPTER 1

I was born in 1632, in the city of York in northern England. My father was a merchant who had become quite wealthy and had settled on an estate in York. There he married my mother, whose family name was Robinson. I came to be known as Robinson Crusoe.

My father gave me the best education he could. He wished me to become a lawyer and to remain on the family estate, but as long as I could remember, I wanted to go to sea. I longed to sail the seas the whole world over. My father begged me, with tears in his eyes, to stay home. He reminded me of my older brother, who had gone off to be a soldier and had been killed in war. "I have lost one son already," my father said. "Must I lose you as well?"

My father's pleas nearly broke my heart. I promised him I would do as he wished. I became determined to forget about ever going to sea. This determination lasted only a few days, though. Soon I was yearning for the sea again. I decided I must run away from home.

So on the first day of September 1651, at the age of eighteen, I left for London with a friend, on board his father's ship. It was then that my troubles started.

The wind began to blow, and the waves rose. I, who had never been at sea, became very ill. I thought heaven was punishing me for running away from my parents. But soon this storm was over, and our sailing was easy.

On the sixth day the wind blew again. The waves rose higher and higher. At first the ship's captain did not seem concerned, but the storm raged harder and harder. Huge waves smashed against the ship. The faces of the captain and the crew were pale. More than once I heard the captain praying in his cabin next to mine. "Lord, have mercy on us," he said. "We shall all be lost."

And I heard some of the crew say this was the worst storm they had ever seen.

One day as I lay in my bunk, the ship tossing in the waves, a sailor shook me awake. "Hurry!" he said. "The ship is leaking! We need everyone to help pump the water out."

Quickly I followed him down to the hold. There we worked like madmen, but the sea came in faster than we could pump it out. The ship would soon sink. Up on the deck, the captain fired a gun as a signal of distress. A gunshot aboard a ship means "Help!"

Another ship, nearby and closer to shore, heard our signal. Soon a boat was sent to us and carried us from our sinking ship. We all struggled to shore in the boat. How we made it in those furious waves we could not guess, but now we were safe.

The leaders of the town were very kind. They found us rooms in which to stay and gave us money to buy food. All we had was lost in the ship. After resting there for a few days, we set out for London.

CHAPTER 2

In London I met another shipmaster. This man had been to the coast of Guinea, where he had made a lot of money by trading. He asked me to sail with him to Guinea. There, he said, I could make my fortune by doing a little simple trading. I agreed at once, and we soon set sail.

We became good friends very quickly. I had never known a man so kind and so honest. He taught me everything he could about navigation and mathematics. Under his teaching, I became a fairly good sailor. And in Guinea, I did indeed make a small fortune with the few things I traded there. When we set sail for London again, I had three hundred pounds (about seven hundred dollars—more than ten years' wages in the seventeenth century) in gold dust.

But, alas, my new friend became ill and died shortly after our return to London. My heart was sick. I had lost my only real friend.

The command of his ship now belonged to his first mate. This man asked me to make another trip to Guinea with him, and I agreed. I took only a third of my money, leaving the rest with the captain's widow.

This voyage, though, was the beginning of my worst troubles in life. We sailed past the coast of Africa. Just as we neared the Canary Islands one gray, cloudy morning, a Turkish pirate ship surprised us from out of the mist. Though we tried to escape, theirs was the lighter ship. They were soon upon us. Our ship had twelve guns; theirs, eighteen. We fought them off as long as we could, but there were just too many of them. Finally they swarmed aboard our ship. We were all taken prisoners.

We were brought into the port of Morocco to be sold as slaves, but the pirate captain kept me. I was young and knew how to sail. He wanted me to work on his ship, so I became the slave of a pirate captain.

This pirate loved to go fishing. Often he would take another slave and me out to sea, and we would fish all day. We went out in the ship the pirates had captured from my old captain friend. As the days and weeks and months passed, I watched and waited for my chance to escape. One day that chance came.

My master had begun to have me take the ship out myself. One day, he ordered me to take three of his friends fishing. We loaded the ship with extra supplies for these guests. Because the men wanted to shoot as well as fish, three casks of gunpowder were among the supplies. When all was ready, my master came to the ship and said that only one of his friends had come. The others were going to be a few days late. He told me to sail that day even though he had some other business and would not be going with us. So the man, the other slave, and I sailed out to sea on a calm, sunny day. *Today is my chance,* I told myself.

I pretended not to catch any fish. When I hooked one, I let it go when the man was not looking. "We will catch nothing here," I said.

"We must go farther out from the shore, where there are more fish." The man agreed. I sailed out to about a mile from shore.

Then, as the pirate stood by the railing of the ship looking out to sea, I came up behind him and shoved him overboard. I then grabbed one of the rifles and pointed it at him as he tried to swim back to the ship. "If you try to come back on board I will shoot you," I said. "Now swim. You are not so far from shore that you cannot make it."

He cursed at me and began swimming. He swam strongly, so I was sure he soon would reach the shore. Now I turned to the other slave, whose name was Xury. "If you swear to be loyal to me, I will take you with me," I said. But if you try to betray me, I will throw you overboard, too."

"I will go the whole world over with you," he said. "I will never betray you as long as I live."

So we sailed straight out to sea. I had hoped the man I threw overboard would watch the direction I took so he would tell his friend, the pirate captain. Then when we were out of sight of the coast, I turned the ship to the east and went under full sail all that day and through the night. The sea was calm and the wind was steady, so by the next day we were about a hundred and fifty miles from Morocco. I kept the sails up for fear of being captured again, and we sailed like this for five days.

Now the wind shifted to the south, and soon we spotted land. As we drew near, I could see that these were the Canary Islands. We dropped anchor near the mouth of a river and went ashore to refill our fresh water supply.

Then we sailed again, heading south along the coasts of these islands.

CHAPTER 3

We sailed south for twenty days, only going ashore whenever we needed fresh water. I hoped to reach the Cape de Verde. I knew that all European trading ships passed that point, and there I hoped to meet one of them.

As we reached this cape, we did indeed see a ship. Xury was terrified, thinking it was one of my old master's ships sent to capture us. I looked at it through a telescope and saw by its flag that it was a Portuguese ship. But it was a long way off and not sailing in our direction. We set full sail, trying to catch up with it before we lost it forever. As we drew near, I fired a gun, hoping they might see the smoke. This worked, for the ship turned to and stopped. In about three hours, we caught up with it and were taken on board. I told them of my capture and slavery and of my escape.

I offered the captain any of my possessions as payment for carrying me with him, but he refused. "I have saved your life only as I would wish to be saved myself if I were in your condition," he said. "Besides, when we reach Brazil you will need your things there to pay your way. You will be a long way from home."

This captain bought my small ship and some of the things I had on it, and he paid me very generously. When we arrived at Brazil, I had two hundred pieces of eight (gold pieces).

The other slave, Xury, wanted to stay with the captain of this ship. I went alone to work on a sugar plantation owned by one of the captain's friends. After several months, I sent for half the money I had left in London. I found a piece of land I was able to buy and started my own plantation.

While living in Brazil for almost four years, I learned the language and made friends with my fellow plantation owners and with many merchants who came into the port. In our talks, I often mentioned how easy it was to trade English goods in Guinea. The natives there paid gold dust for trinkets such as beads, knives, scissors, and bits of glass.

One day, three of my merchant friends came to me, said they wished to sail to Guinea, and asked me to come with them. They said if I would manage the trading, they would give me an equal share of the profits. Though I already had everything I could ever want, I could not resist this offer. I left my estate in the hands of my servants, wrote my will, leaving everything I owned to the good Portuguese captain in case anything happened to me, and set out.

On the first day of September 1659, eight years to the day since I left my father and my mother, I set sail with my friends, bound for Guinea. We followed a northward course toward the African coast. On the twelfth day a violent storm blew up. The winds changed from southeast to northwest to northeast, blowing our ship off course with each change. The waves pounded our ship for twelve days before the storm finally let up. One man was washed overboard during the storm.

Now the captain took a sighting and discovered that we were off the northern coast of Brazil, beyond the Amazon River. The captain asked me what we should do. The ship was leaking, and we could not make it to Guinea without making some repairs and replenishing our food supply. We decided to follow the shortest course, which would be to the island of Bardados, about fifteen days away. So we set our course northwest by west.

But soon another storm hit us. This one drove us off course to the west for many days. We knew there were no civilized lands in this direction.

One morning the lookout shouted, "Land!" We had no sooner run out of our cabins to look than the ship struck sand. It stuck fast, and the huge waves washed over the decks. The captain called all together—eleven of us—and said that we must abandon ship. "This pounding of these waves will break the ship into pieces," he said. "Our only hope is to make it to shore in our boat."

So we prayed for God's mercy, lowered the boat into the sea, and climbed aboard. We soon realized the waves were much higher than we had thought. We rowed toward shore for all we were worth. The boat climbed mountains of waves and plunged down the other sides, again and again. One such wave was too much for our boat. Suddenly we were all dumped into the sea, as the boat disappeared under the raging waters.

I felt myself carried toward shore by the wave. When it

spent itself out and went back, my feet were on ground. Now I began running toward shore through the shallow water. I hoped to reach the shore before the next wave crashed down on me. But the shore was still a long way off. Another wave hit me, submerging me in thirty or forty feet of water, and rushed me onward toward the shore. Just as I thought I could hold my breath no longer, my head shot above the surface. It was just for an instant, but enough for me to take a deep breath before I was plunged back under the water. Finally this wave had washed itself out, and I was much nearer the shore. I struggled onward, my strength failing me, my legs becoming like lead weights.

But still I could not outrun the waves. Another crashed down on me and carried me on with it until my lungs were ready to burst. Finally I was able to struggle clear and, as the wave went back, I found my feet and slogged onward. This time I reached the shore. I clambered up a little hill and lay panting on the grass. The waves crashed onto the shore behind me.

As I lay there, I wondered frantically what had happened to my companions. But I would never again see any of them.

Now I got to my feet and walked along the shore. Where was I? What dangers awaited me here? A forest lay along the shore. Did any people live there? What sort of wild beasts were there?

Night was coming fast. I had only a knife. Struggling to

stay awake as I walked, I went to the forest edge and climbed a thick, bushy tree, like a fir tree but thorny. I lay on one of its thick branches and fell fast asleep.

CHAPTER 4

When I awoke, the weather was clear and the sea, calm. I was surprised to see that the ship had been driven off the sand bar and stood out of the shallow water only about a mile from shore.

A little after noon, the tide was low enough that I could walk to within a quarter mile of the ship. Now I realized, with grief that made my tears flow, that if we had all stayed aboard, no one would have drowned.

I swam the remaining distance to the ship and climbed aboard. The stern (rear) was facing the shore, resting on the sand. The bow (front) was pitching down into the water. The living quarters were at the rear, so this area had stayed dry. I searched for anything I might be able to use on shore.

I found bread, rice, cheese, water, clothes, tools, rifles, pistols, ammunition and gunpowder, two rusty swords, and many other things. I gathered as much as I could onto the deck, but then I thought—how was I to get these things to shore?

I had to build a raft. I found some spare topmasts (like posts), several planks, and some rope. Throwing all this overboard, I jumped in after it and tied the masts together. Then I laid the planks across them and tied them on. I kept working on it, adding bracing and rope, until it seemed strong enough to carry me and a heavy load. Then I carefully loaded it with as much as it could carry and shoved off for shore.

As it was now late afternoon, the tide was going in. This carried me to shore. I spied a little river that the sea washed into and steered my raft toward this, thinking to come inland a bit. I went up this river until I saw a likely spot to set up camp—a high, flat area on one bank.

I tied the raft down here. Now I needed to explore, to find out what sort of place I was in. I loaded a rifle and a pistol and set out for a tall, steep hill about a mile away. At the top, I saw my fate. I was on an island with no land in sight all around except two small islands about three leagues (nine miles) to the west.

I went back to the raft and began unloading my cargo. This took the rest of that day. I made a sort of hut by piling boxes up around me and covering them with sailcloth. Night came on. I was afraid to sleep in this place, not knowing what sort of wild beasts might live here. I kept my loaded guns next to me that night and slept with no trouble.

The next day I went back to the ship. I needed to bring away as much as I could. Anything might be useful to me, and I had no idea how long I might have to stay here. I was also afraid that the ship might drift off to sea before I could get all I needed from it. So every day, for almost two weeks, I rummaged through the ship, loading everything I could find onto my raft. I brought bags of nails, tools, a dozen hatchets, a grindstone, clothes, sails, a bed, rope, twine, cables, a barrel of flour—anything I could fit on my raft.

On the thirteenth day it grew overcast, and the wind blew in from the sea. I stayed in my hut, surrounded by piles and piles of my loot. The wind howled all that day and night.

When I looked out the next day, the ship was gone. It had been driven off by the wind and the waves. I was very glad I had wasted no time in emptying the ship before it was lost to me. I had enough, I thought, to survive here a long time if I had to.

But now, I would have to move because the ground I camped on was marshy. I needed solid ground and a strong shelter, safe from wild beasts or savage natives. With my guns in hand, I went searching for a good place, found a little grassy plain at the foot of a cliff overlooking the sea. In one part of the cliff was a shallow cave. I decided to build here. I could build a fort with this cliff to my back and hollow out the cave to use as a storeroom.

I first drew a half-circle about ten yards out from the cliff wall and about twenty yards across. Around this half-circle I drove two rows of strong stakes. Then I laid layers of cable, which I had cut from the ship, between these two rows. I made a roof of branches and covered it with canvas sails from the ship. The dirt and stones that I dug out of the cave I piled up in front of my outer wall. This made an earthen bank all over my fort. From a distance it could not be seen as a dwelling, but looked like part of the cliff itself. Into this "house," I brought all my things from the ship and, little by little, arranged them to my liking. I made wooden shelves in the cave at my back, where I stored my gunpowder and anything else that needed to stay dry.

Now, all this took a long time. I had to cut trees from the forest in order to build. I had some tools, but not everything I needed. I had to invent many things as I went. I worked on this house for about a year and a half.

During this time, I took a gun with me daily to hunt for food. I had discovered goats on the island. They were very wary of me, and it was difficult for me to get close enough to shoot them. But I learned that if I came to them from over the cliffs, and they were below me, they did not see me. So in this way I was able to shoot one whenever I needed meat.

Two cats and a dog from the ship were now my only companions. I began to wonder if I would live out my life here alone and die alone. I made a calendar, a simple post into which I cut a notch for each day, to keep track of the passing days. Every seventh day I rested, as on the Sabbath. I had also salvaged paper and ink from the ship, and I started to keep a diary to pass the time.

At times, my loneliness seemed too great a burden to bear. With tears streaming down my face, I cried out to heaven, "Why have I been so abandoned?"

One day, as I walked along the shore, a new thought came to me. Yes, I was alone here, but I was indeed alive. I had been saved from the sea while the other ten men had all drowned.

Then I thought, *I have all I need here to live comfortably. And how was it that the ship had been driven toward the shore and had stayed there long enough for me to get from it all I needed? Was all that just chance?*

I thought about these things and thought about them, until it occurred to me that in even the most miserable conditions there is comfort; in despair there is yet hope. For every evil there is a better good. With these thoughts, I began to feel more at peace on my island. I began almost to enjoy my life here.

CHAPTER 5

In November, more than a year after I was shipwrecked, my days began to fall into a regular order. My home was nearly completed. In the mornings, I went hunting for two or three hours before working for another couple of hours on my house. Then I would eat my midday meal before taking a nap in the early afternoon. It was very hot during that part of the day.

I kept the skins of every animal I shot. These I dried in the sun and used as rugs and coverings and, eventually, to make clothes.

I made a table and a chair and continued to expand the size of my cave storeroom. With my rough furniture and my shelves filled with things, I began to feel quite at home in my little fort. One day, I was nearly buried when the roof of my cave fell in. It seemed that I had made it too big. After I cleared all the dirt out, I braced up the ceiling with a few stray posts with boards laid across the tops.

One day in December, I shot a goat but only crippled it by hitting it in the leg. Instead of killing it, I decided to take it home. I made a splint for its leg and cared for it until it was well again. Now it was quite tame and stayed with me, my dog, and my cats who were no longer two, but a whole family.

This was the first time I thought of breeding my own

goats, like cattle, so I would have food when my gunpowder was gone, and I could no longer hunt. That would be quite some time yet, but I was learning to plan ahead for everything.

One day, as I was looking through my things, I found a little bag that had been filled with barley. There was no grain now, only husks and dust, because the rats on the ship had eaten the grain. But I wanted the bag, so I threw the dust out near my home.

About a month later, I noticed some little green shoots growing where I had thrown the barley dust. In a few weeks they had grown taller, and now tiny corns of barley appeared. I could hardly believe my eyes. Here, in a climate not suited for grain, from worthless dust I had thrown away, were growing perfect, healthy stalks of barley. Then to my astonishment, I saw another type of plant sprouting near this barley. Rice! I could tell it was rice because I had seen it in Africa.

Strangely enough, this was the first time in my life that I thought of God. These grains growing on this remote island seemed to be a miracle. Could it be that God, in His infinite kindness, had made this grain grow here to provide food for me? This simple thought touched my heart as nothing in my life had before, and it brought tears to my eyes.

Soon after this, something happened that terrified me, and from which I did not recover for a long time. I sat inside my house, just inside the entrance to my cave, when all of a sudden I heard a loud crack as if the whole mountain had split! Then the walls shook, and stones tumbled out of the ceiling.

I quickly climbed outside. Now I could tell that it was an earthquake. The ground shook, the mountain rumbled, and even the sea trembled. A rock as tall as a house that stood a little out to sea cracked in two and fell into the sea with a deafening crash. After several minutes, all was still.

But I was afraid to go back into my house. I sat down, hoping my courage would return. As I sat there, the sky grew dark, the wind began to howl, and the waves of the sea rose, smashing onto the shore. After an hour of this, it grew very still. Then the rain came. It poured down harder than I had ever seen before. I was forced to go inside.

It rained all that night and most of the next day. Inside, I decided that I would not be safe in that cave in another earthquake. I would have to move. This thought filled me with dread. It had been such long, hard work to build this place. I did not look forward to building another. Still, I must, I thought. It must be on open ground, where there was no danger of a mountain falling down on me. Though it would be a long time, I would live here where I was while I worked on another home.

CHAPTER 6

One morning after this last storm I looked out to sea and saw the wrecked ship again. It had been driven in closer to the shore. I went out to it at low tide and found it all choked with sand. There was no getting into it now. But I began pulling pieces off it—planks and timbers and anything I could get. I wanted to take it all away, piece by piece, if I could. Everything might be useful to me someday. This was the first day of May. I kept at this work until the fifteenth of June.

During this time, I had forgotten all about building a new home. When I was finished with the ship, I had enough timber, planking, and ironwork to build a good boat—if only I knew how.

The next day, I found a large sea turtle and spent the rest of the day cooking it. The meat was the best I had ever tasted, and a welcome change from the goats and water birds I had eaten since coming to this island.

A couple of days after this I became ill. I went from cold fits to hot and back to cold. I lay in a fever all day, too weak to move and very frightened because I was so alone with no one to help me. I prayed to God, though I did not really know how to pray.

The next day I was better but very weak. I ate some food

for strength and rested all day. Again the next day I was very ill. The fits became so violent I was sure I would die. "Lord, look upon me!" I cried. "Lord, have mercy on me!" I went on like this for two or three hours until I fell asleep.

When I awoke, I felt better. I was very thirsty but too weak to get up for water. So I just went to sleep again.

This illness lasted for many days. Some days I felt well enough to get up and eat. Other days I could only lie in my hammock. I was afraid I would die.

I had much time to think, as I could do nothing else. And I thought of God again. My memory went back over my life, back to my father teaching me about God and about good things. I remembered running away from my parents. Now I realized that for all these years that I had been away from home, I had done just as I pleased, with not one thought for God or anyone else. *Am I being punished now for ignoring God?* I wondered. I realized, too, that in all the fortunate things that had happened to me—my escape from the pirate captain, my wealth from trading, my successful sugar plantation, my escape from the sea—in all these I had not once recognized God's hand in my life. Not once had I thanked Him. And all the while I was on this island, I had been hoping for deliverance from this lonely life. I had overlooked my deliverance from the sea in the shipwreck.

When I awoke on the twenty-eighth of June, the fever had left me, but I was still very weak. I spent this day just resting and eating a little food when I could. That afternoon I sat on the beach and watched the sea. I found that my thoughts were still on God.

Who made the sea? I wondered. *And the earth and sky? And me?* Surely God did. If He made everything, then He must guide and govern everything as He wishes. If so, then it was His wish to save me from the sea, to provide for me so well on this island. I had not yet given one thought to it.

That night I picked up a Bible I had saved from the ship. The first words I read when I opened it were from Psalm 50:15: "Call upon me in the day of trouble: I will deliver thee, and thou shalt glorify me." Thinking of these words, I fell asleep.

When I awoke, I was very refreshed and hungry. I stayed around my house resting, thinking, and walking a little. My thoughts were constantly on the words, "I will deliver thee." Then it occurred to me that God had delivered me from this illness. This touched my heart. I knelt down and thanked Him.

After this, I read my Bible every morning and night, thinking deeply about what I read. And the more I read, the more I thought of my sinful life. My guilt became so heavy I thought I would die of grief. Then one day I came to the words, "Him hath God exalted with his right hand to be a Prince and a Savior, for to give repentance to Israel, and forgiveness of sins." I threw down the Bible, lifted my hands to heaven, and cried, "Jesus, exalted prince and Savior, give me repentance and forgiveness!"

This was the first real prayer I had ever prayed. It came from deep within my heart, and I knew, I just knew, that the Lord had heard me. Now for the first time I understood the promise of deliverance. It was not deliverance from this island, or of anything else in life, but deliverance from my own sinful self and from my guilt.

Now as the days passed, and as I continued to read the Bible and to pray, a peace grew in my heart, such a peace as I had never known before. I had found God.

On the fifteenth day of July, I went up the river where I had first brought my raft. I wanted to explore my island. I found that the ocean tide went up this river about two miles, and after that the water was fresh and good. There was very little of it now, though, as this was the dry season.

On the banks I found many smooth, grass-covered meadows. Here grew wild tobacco, aloes, sugarcane, and many other plants I did not recognize. This was as far as I went that day before returning to my seaside home.

The next day, I went farther upstream. Past the meadows, the land became more wooded. Here lime, lemon, and orange trees flourished along with melons and grapes. When night came, I climbed a tree and slept there.

The next day, I traveled about four miles farther into this area and came to an opening where the country sloped downhill to the west. Everything was lush and green and beautiful, as if it had been planted as a garden. I saw now that I had made my home on the worst side of this island.

I stayed here the rest of the day, picking bunches of grapes and laying the vines over tree branches to dry in the sun. I had decided to make these dried grapes, or raisins, to eat during the next rainy season, when it was hard to find food. And I picked as many lemons and limes as I could carry. I would have to return to my home and bring some bags to carry everything.

My journey home and back took three days. I got what I needed and returned to this pleasant, green place. Here I spent the rest of the month of July, building a kind of bower with stakes set in a circle, interwoven with branches.

In August the rains started to fall. I had to return to my side of the island. I gathered as many of the now-dried grapes and the lemons and limes as I could carry and came home to my cave-house.

It rained every day from the middle of August until the middle of October. I had to stay indoors most of this time. I was very glad for my raisins and citrus fruits.

While indoors, I began to dig in my cave to make a back doorway to my house. I dug a pathway to one side and turned and came out at the cliff wall. As soon as I did this, I wondered if I should have such an opening that I could not guard. Still, I had seen nothing on the island worse than a goat. I was sure there were no dangerous beasts here.

All this time, I had kept count of the passing days on my post-calendar. I decided to make the thirtieth of September, the anniversary of my landing here, a day of giving thanks to God. I spent the day praying and fasting (going without food).

When the rains stopped in October, I returned to my bower on the other side of the island. I was astonished to see that the stakes I had cut from trees were sprouting branches. This was a wonderful discovery. As they grew, I cut and pruned them. (In three years, they would form a shaded roof over my bower.)

Seeing this, I cut more of these stakes and placed them around my home by the sea. These, too, would grow into trees in a few years.

When the spring rains were over, I decided to go to the other side of my island. This time I would go all the way to the seashore. I took my gun, a hatchet, my dog, biscuit cakes, and bunches of raisins and started out.

The sky was very clear when I came within view of the sea on the west side. As I looked out over the water, I saw land. I could not tell if it was part of a continent, or just another island, but it was very wide. I judged that it was about twenty leagues (sixty miles) away. Island or continent, it was much too far for me to sail to in anything but a ship or very large boat.

Flocks of parrots lived on this side of my island. I decided to catch one and tame it, so I could teach it to speak. I did manage to catch a young one by knocking it down with a stick, but it would be years before he began to speak.

Here, too, were hundreds of sea turtles and many kinds of waterfowl. I decided that I had indeed built my home on the wrong side of this island. I walked toward the east along the seashore for about twelve miles. Then I set up a marker, a tall post, and returned. I wanted to walk from the other direction, from my home, to see how long it would take to reach this marker. That would give me an idea of the size of my island.

On my journey home, my dog caught a kid (young goat). I saved the kid before my dog could hurt it and took it home with me. Perhaps I could start my own flock with this kid, I thought. My first pet goat had died earlier of mere old age. Now my family had grown. I had the cats, the dog, a goat, and a parrot, whom I named Poll.

The autumn rainy season was now upon me. On the thirtieth of September, I again spent the day in prayer and fasting. I thanked God for making my life here happy and comfortable. I thanked Him because I now realized that here, on this lonely island, my life was better than it had been in my past sinful life. Here I had everything I needed to live in peace and contentment. God had changed my very heart, giving me new, simpler desires.

I still read my Bible daily. It gave me much comfort. One morning, feeling particularly lonely and sad, I opened it to the words, "I will never leave thee, nor forsake thee." This, I realized, was spoken directly to me. "Well, then," I said, "if God does not forsake me, what does it matter if the whole world has forsaken me? And what would it be to me if I had all the world, if I should lose the favor of God?"

It was with these thoughts that I began my third year on the island. My days were now very ordered. The first thing in the morning, I read my Bible and prayed. Then I ate breakfast, usually raisins. Then I hunted for a few hours before eating my midday meal. I rested in the afternoon as it was too hot to go out. Everything I made took a very long time because of my simple tools and lack of skills. But work was pleasant. It kept me occupied, and, indeed, it seemed I had all the time in the world.

There were two rainy seasons each year, in the spring and in the fall. These would last about two months each. During those times, I stayed inside making baskets out of dried reeds and teaching my parrot to talk.

I planted my barley and rice twice a year, just before each rain season. My harvests grew and grew. Each time I sowed my seed, I thought back to my discovery of the little patch of grain that, it seemed, God had made grow there for me.

CHAPTER 9

What I wanted most on my island was a cooking pot. My only method of cooking meat was roasting. Many times I wished I could make soup or stew. And now that I was harvesting so much barley and rice, I needed some way to cook meal. It was by accident that I learned how to make such a pot.

I had made several small pots out of a clay I found on the beach. These I let bake in the sun until they were hard enough to use, and then I kept dried grains and such in them. But they would never stand to hold boiling water. One day, I roasted some meat over a large fire. When I was finished, and the fire was dying down, I noticed a broken piece of one of my pots in the fire. To my surprise, I saw that it had become hard as stone and burned to a red color. The fire had hardened the piece as if in a pottery kiln. Now I knew how to make my pots!

I made several large pots and put them in a roaring fire. After about six hours, they became glazed and very hard. The sand mixed with the clay had heated so much that it had melted and run like liquid glass, giving the pots a hard, glossy surface. Now, in one of these pots, I boiled some goat meat until it made a nice broth. This was a wonderful discovery.

The next thing I wanted was a bread oven. I had not had

bread for more than two years. For this, I made some bricks of the sand-clay mixture and fired them as I had done the pots. Then I made a wide, shallow dish to lay over the bricks, which themselves were heated by placing them on the coals of a fire.

Making the bread itself was much harder than the oven. I had to separate the husks from the grain by hand, having no sieve or sifter, and this was a very slow process. Later I discovered how to make sieves from some neckcloths made of calico that I had saved from the ship. But eventually I had bread, though flat cakes instead of nice loaves, because I had no yeast. All of this took me a third of a year, and I worked at it during the rainy seasons.

Now, more and more, my thoughts were on that land I had seen from the western side of my island. I wished I could sail to it. Perhaps there would be other people there, and perhaps I could make my way from there back to England. I would need a very big boat to sail to that land, I knew. I began searching the island for a tree out of which I could make a big canoe. I had seen the natives in Brazil make a canoe of a single tree by burning and scraping out the inside. This was how I would make my boat.

I found a tree that was about six feet in diameter at the bottom and well over twenty feet tall. I spent twenty days hacking with my axe before it fell and fourteen more taking off the branches. Then I spent almost three more months shaping it to look something like the bottom of a boat, though very roughly, and cleaning out the inside with a mallet and chisel.

When I was done, I had a canoe big enough to carry more than two dozen men. I was very proud. But then and only then did I wonder how I was to get it into the water. It lay about a hundred yards from the shore. I could not begin to move it myself. It may seem odd that I had not thought of this at first, but it was true. I had only one thought that drove me all the while I worked on the boat—to get to that other shore. Never once did I consider how I would launch my boat once it was made!

Now I tried everything. I began to dig a channel to it, hoping the incoming tide would carry it out. But soon after I started, I realized how much I would have to dig. It would take me more than ten years to dig such a channel! Finally I gave up all efforts to move the boat, and decided to learn from this to be wiser the next time.

Now four years had passed here. The time I spent reading the Bible and praying was changing me. I found that I had no more cares for the world I had known before my life on this island. That past life now seemed to be something from a dream that is hard to remember. Here, alone, I found that I no longer wanted the things I used to want. I had no greed, no selfish ambition, no wrong desires of any sort. Though I had timber enough to build a fleet of ships, and grapes enough to fill those ships with wine, they were nothing to me. I took only what I could use, and that was very little. I had learned to live in harmony with the world God made. Daily I gave thanks for my daily bread.

Many things I had saved from the ship were long gone now. My ink was gone, so I could no longer keep a journal. And my clothes were badly worn. I needed something that would last longer than the linen garments from the ship. As I said earlier in my story, I had saved the skins from every animal I killed. Some of these were too stiff for use, but others were soft. During the rainy seasons, I sat inside sewing these skins into clothes. Slowly, and crudely, I worked them into shape. I made a hat, a vest, pants that came to my knees, and an umbrella. I left the hair on these garments, so they shed water when it rained. The umbrella was best of all. Under its shade I could now go out during the hottest part of the day and stay cool and comfortable.

During my fifth year, I made another canoe, smaller than the first. This time I made it near the river so I could easily launch it.

CHAPTER 10

Now I knew this canoe was much too small to sail to the other land. My only thought was to sail around my island. I made a mast and sail and tried it along the shore. It worked very well. So one day, I put some food aboard and started out, hoping to go around the island.

But when I came to the east side I was stopped. There a ledge of rocks went out into the sea for about two leagues (six miles). I would have to sail far out into the sea to go around it. I landed and climbed a hill to see what lay on the other side of this ledge. From the hill, I could see a strong current running to the east just past the end of the rocks. I realized that if I got into that current, I could be carried far out to sea. I would have to stay close to the rocks to get around them.

But as the sea was calm, and as there was no wind, I decided to round this ledge of rocks. Just as I reached the point, though, I found my canoe in very deep water in a powerful current. The current was closer to the point than I had thought! Now I was being carried helplessly out to sea.

Oh, why had I been so foolish as to sail so far from shore! Now I looked back at my island, which appeared smaller and smaller as I rushed away from it. In despair, I worked feverishly with my oar to keep the canoe as close as possible to the edge of the current.

Soon I felt a little breeze in my face. With that breeze came a little hope. I could barely see the island now. The breeze grew steadily until it was quite a strong gale. Now I raised my sail and slowly, steadily passed out of the current. I was safe!

The gale blew steadily toward the shore, taking my canoe with it. In an hour I was safe on shore again. I jumped out of the canoe and fell on my knees, thanking God for His deliverance. I swore I would never again take to the sea in my canoe.

I found a little cove and paddled my canoe into it. Here I could leave the canoe. I discovered I was near the place where I had left my marker on the beach. Now it was easy for me to find my way up the hills to my summer "estate," where I had built my bower. I entered this bower, ate some supper, and fell asleep.

It was night and all was still. I slept soundly after my tiring adventure with the canoe. Some time in the night I was startled awake by the sound of a voice. *A voice! I must have been dreaming,* I thought. But then, fully awake, I heard it again. "Robin, poor Robin Crusoe. Where are you, Robin Crusoe?" I was terrified. Who, or what, could this be on my island, and knowing my name, too?

Just then a big bird fluttered down from the roof of the bower and landed on my arm. "Poor Robin Crusoe, where have you been?" it said.

Poll! It was my pet parrot, whom I had taught to speak. How he had found me here I could not guess. But here he was, and I was glad to see him! We went together the next day, Poll on my arm, back to our seaside home.

I was now in my eleventh year on the island. As my gun-powder supply was getting low, I thought again of breeding tame goats so I would have meat when I could no longer hunt. I would need to get more goats for this. I had only my one pet goat. I decided to try to trap some.

First, I made several types of snares, but none worked. The goats were too clever for any of them. Then I dug large pits, covered them lightly with small branches, and set food on them as bait. The next day, I found three kids inside one of the pits. I tied these together and took them home. They soon became quite tame as I fed them daily.

But then it occurred to me that I needed to keep the tame ones separate from the wild ones, or I would not be able to keep any goats with me. So I had to begin building a fence. I did this with the same stakes I had used to make my bower and my home. I closed in an area about a hundred yards by a hundred and fifty yards. This took almost three months. My first three goats were very content here. They had grass for grazing and a little stream of water.

In about a year and a half, I had twelve goats. In two more years, I had forty-three. I made more pastures as my flocks increased, driving the goats from one to another as I needed to. And eventually, I learned to milk them and to make butter and cheese.

How wonderful is God, Who had supplied me with such riches on this remote island!

CHAPTER 11

One day I decided to visit my canoe on the other side of the island. I wanted to go along the shore, as I had not gone this way yet. As I walked, I smiled to think of how I would appear to someone on the streets of England. I would be quite a sight. I wore the clothes I described earlier and carried my umbrella. I also wore a wide belt of goatskin, from which hung a hatchet and a little saw. Across one shoulder I wore another belt, from which hung one bag of gunshot and one of powder. I kept my beard trimmed to a fairly short length with scissors I had gotten from the ship. I went barefoot, the long goat hair from my pants hanging down to my shins.

It was about noon when I came near the little cove where my boat lay. But I never reached the boat. What I saw next I shall never forget. It was the most terrifying thing that had ever happened to me. There just before me in the sand, clearly outlined, was the print of a man's naked foot!

I looked up and down the beach to see if there were more tracks, but there was only this one. Shaking with terror, I turned and ran all the way back to my seaside home.

I huddled in my cave for three days before I dared to come out. Those three days were a living nightmare of fear. *Who made that print? How did he get to my island? Why were there no other prints? Is it a man or a devil? How many of them are there? Have they discovered my goat pastures? My boat?*

In my mind, I saw hordes of naked savages roaming over my island, searching for me to kill and eat me. I had heard of cannibals, people who eat other people, living in the Caribbean Islands, where I might very well be right now.

In my fear, I did not once think of God, my protector. Instead, I foolishly began to think of ways to protect myself. At first, I thought I should destroy my fenced-in pastures, my grain field, and everything else I had made, so no one would think a man was living here. I had many more such thoughts but sat hiding in my cave, too afraid to act on any of them.

Early one morning as I lay in my hammock thinking these evil thoughts, the words of that first Scripture I had read years ago came back to me. "Call upon me in the day of trouble: I will deliver thee, and thou shalt glorify me" (Psalm 50:15). Suddenly I felt hope. I got on my knees and prayed. Then I opened my Bible, and the first words I read were, "Wait on the LORD: be of good courage, and he sha' ngthen thine heart" (Psalm 27:14).

I cannot ever describe the comfor' the hope. The Lord had delivered me f sea more than once. Could He nc new danger? With a sense of sh times the fear of danger is ter than the danger itself.

I went out about my now. I decided to do v

from enemies if they ever came to my island again. I made the wall of my house stronger by adding more stakes and earth until it was so thick that nothing could have gotten through it. I made seven small holes in the wall. In each of these I placed a loaded musket, like cannon surrounding a fort. And all around my house, in every direction, I planted stake after stake, probably twenty thousand. When they sprouted, they made a forest so thick it was impassable.

Planting this forest took nearly two years. In all that time I saw no more trace of anyone on the island.

CHAPTER 12

My life on the island had changed. Now I did everything with caution, if not fear. I had to be careful not to make smoke when I cooked with fire. I no longer chopped wood, for fear of the noise my axe made; now I used my saw. I lived with the constant fear that any day I might be captured and devoured by savages. Now when I prayed, it was not with such a merry heart as before. Instead, I prayed for protection and comfort. (I have since learned from this that an attitude of thankfulness and worship is the right one for prayer, not fear and worry.)

It was more than two years after seeing the man's print that I made my next discovery of man on the island. This discovery was much more horrifying than the first.

I had gone to the western side of the island to check my drying grapes. From there, I decided to go down to the seashore. On the shore I came across the remains of a cannibal feast. Human skulls and other bones lay scattered about a large cooking pit dug in the sand. I was so shocked at this, I did not even consider my own danger. I just wanted to get as far away as I could from that terrible scene.

Now anger stirred in me. I would kill all those wicked savages, I thought. And, if possible, I would save their victims, whom they brought here to eat. I found a place among some trees where I could hide and shoot at them on the beach.

I loaded several guns and went in the morning to this hiding place. There I waited all day. I did this daily for over three months. All that time I saw no one.

I soon grew tired of this. And as my anger wore off, I began to think other thoughts. What was I planning to do? Murder these savages? I had not thought of it in that way before now. But now I realized their cannibal feasts were not acts of murder. To those savages, killing and eating their enemies were no different than my killing and eating the goats on my island. Those people were not committing willful murder. They were only doing what they had done for ages. They knew no better. Was I better than they by planning to shoot them for a "crime" they had no idea they were committing?

I decided it was not for me to judge them. I must avoid them, but I could not shoot them unless they first attacked me. I decided to stay away from that part of the island.

I went about my business on the other side of the island, always keeping my guns with me, and always alert for danger. But I felt a little more at ease with my situation. I realized that the natives who came to the western side would have no reason to come over to this side. They probably came there when they went out to sea too far from their land and were driven off course to this island. They would have no desire to stay here, I told myself. But, even so, I often wished I had some place of safety where I could go if I were in danger, a secret place where I could not be found. One day I made a discovery that was far better than what I had wished for.

I had moved all my cooking and pot-making from my seaside home to my bower in the woods, where the smoke could be lost in the trees and not seen. One day, I was sawing wood at the foot of a small hill in the forest. As I reached for a piece of wood, I noticed a hollow place in the hill, under a thick tree branch. I crawled under the branches into a hole and, to my wonder, soon found myself in a cave large enough to stand in. Quickly, I went back to my bower and got some wax candles and crawled back into the hole.

Now I discovered that the cave was about twelve feet across. I walked to the back wall and there saw another hole in which I could see only darkness. Holding my candle, I crawled into this hole. After about ten yards, it came out into a large inner cave. I stood up, held up my light, and gasped in wonder.

The ceiling here was about twenty feet high. The floor was dry and smooth, covered with loose gravel. And on the walls, in the yellow light of my candle, glittered thousands of sparkling jewels. I stood there marveling at the sight and rejoicing in my discovery.

That day, I brought two fowling pieces (like shotguns), three muskets, and a barrel of gunpowder to this inner cave. This was the retreat I had wanted, a place no one would ever be likely to discover.

In December of my twenty-third year on the island, I went out to my fields to harvest my grain. Early in the morning, before the sun was up, I came out of my grove of trees on the shore and stopped cold. I had seen fire. Or so I thought. I crept forward and peered down the beach. Yes, there was a fire. It was about two miles off. I felt dread. Now the savages were on my side of the island!

I rushed into my cave, made sure all my muskets were loaded, and sat, waiting. For what? I did not know. I prayed for protection. Finally I could not bear to wait any longer. I had to see what was happening.

I climbed to the top of the cliff that overlooked my house. Here I lay flat and looked through my telescope. I saw nine savages sitting around a large fire. Two canoes were hauled up onto the shore. The tide was out. I wondered if they were waiting for the tide to return before they left.

I watched them for more than an hour. When they were done eating, they danced around the fire. And, as I had guessed, when the tide came in, they left in their canoes. When they had gone a good distance out, I started down to their campsite.

What a horror! Blood and bones and uneaten flesh lay about. I was so filled with repulsion and fury, I decided I would destroy the next group who came, no matter how large.

But they did not come again soon, at least not to my knowledge. It would be more than three years before I saw any again.

Meanwhile, a year and three months after this discovery, something else happened that made me quite forget all about the savages for awhile.

It was in May of my twenty-fifth year. A fierce storm had been blowing all day and all through that night. I sat inside my house reading my Bible. Suddenly I was startled by the sound of a gunshot. Quickly, I climbed out of my house onto the cliff and lay waiting. There it came again, out to sea. It must be a ship in distress. I could tell by the sound that the ship must lie near the point of the rock ledge, where I had been driven to sea in my canoe.

I gathered dry wood from my storeroom and made a big fire on the cliff. It blazed up into the night. Surely the men on the ship could see it. I kept the fire going until, there, another gunshot, then several more came.

The next day was clear. I looked through my telescope and saw something out to sea but could not see what it was. I went around to the place where the rock ledge went out from the beach, and I looked again. This time I saw clearly. It was a ship, wrecked on the rocks. Sadly, I wondered what had happened. Perhaps they had seen my light, had gotten into a boat to come to me, and had been driven out to sea by that current. I thought I should go to the ship to see if anyone was still aboard. But I did not dare try that current again.

I climbed the hill from which I could see the point of the rock ledge. I saw the current as before, on the south side of the island. But then I noticed another current, going toward the island on the north side. These currents must shift often, I thought. I had not seen that one before. Now I knew that even if I got caught in the outgoing current, I could just let myself drift until I hit the other current on the north side, and so return safely.

So I got out my canoe and sailed out to the ship, about four miles. It was a Spanish ship, stuck fast in the rocks. The stern (rear) was broken to pieces. As I came close, a dog appeared on the deck. When I called to him, he jumped into my canoe. He was nearly starved. I gave him a cake and some water. Then I climbed aboard the ship.

In the cookroom were two men, drowned, their arms about each other. There was no one else aboard. But I was delighted to find some things I could use. There were several muskets, a barrel of powder, a fire shovel and tongs, brass kettles and pots, several fine linen shirts, and best of all, four pairs of leather shoes.

I also took some glass bottles and several bags of gold pieces. There was nothing else I wanted, so I loaded my canoe and sailed back to shore.

I took these things to my secret cave in the woods. I cared

nothing for the gold, but stashed it inside just on the hope that if I ever got off the island and back to England, it would be useful to me then. The shoes, though, were the real treasures. I had gone barefoot here for many years.

CHAPTER 14

It was about two years later that I had my first encounter with the savages.

One morning, I saw five canoes on my beach about a mile away. I could not tell how many men were on the beach. I guessed thirty. With my loaded guns, I climbed to my cliff-top and spied on them with my telescope. There were indeed thirty or more, dancing around a roaring fire. Now they dragged two men from one of the canoes. They clubbed one of these, leaving the other standing. Now the one standing saw his chance and sprinted away. And could he run! He came in my direction. Two others chased him, but they were not nearly as fast as he.

Between them and me was a narrow inlet of water. The man running did not slow down on reaching this, but dived in and swam across in about thirty powerful strokes. The other two dived in after him.

I decided I must save this man. I could not bear to watch him be caught and murdered. I ran down the beach toward them. The escaping man saw me, and I waved for him to come to me. He seemed as frightened of me as of them. I came up to the other two now and clubbed one with my rifle butt. He dropped to the sand. The other quickly fit an arrow to his bow. Before he could bring his bow up, I shot him dead.

The man I had saved now came up to me and bowed low to the ground. He spoke words I did not understand. I made gestures to him to show that I was a friend. He seemed to understand.

Now the savage I had clubbed was stirring and sitting up. The man I had saved quickly motioned to me for my sword. I handed it to him, and he rushed over and killed his enemy. Then he came to me, laughing and bowing, and gave me back my sword. I had just gained a friend for life.

We buried the two savages so the others would not find them. Then I led my new friend to my secret cave in the woods. Here I gave him barley cakes and goat's milk. He seemed to enjoy it very much.

After he had eaten, we went back to the beach. The other savages had left. It seemed they were not interested in their escaped captive or their lost companions. I had my man gather up their grisly mess and burn it in a pile.

I gave him my sword, which he already showed he knew how to use well, and a bow and arrows. He was very pleased with these. He was pleased, too, when I gave him a linen shirt and shorts and made him a goatskin cap like mine.

I decided to call him Friday because that was the day, as near as I could tell, that I had rescued him. He was tall and strongly built. I guessed his age to be twenty-six. His nature was the kindest, most loving I had ever known in any man. And he would prove to be the most loyal, worthy companion a man could possibly hope for.

CHAPTER 15

I began to teach Friday to speak English. He learned quickly. Soon we could communicate with a few words and many gestures.

At first he was terrified of my guns. He thought they were alive and that they could kill at will. For many days, I taught him about guns, showing him how they worked and how I could use them to kill animals for food. He learned to tolerate them and eventually to use them himself.

I taught him how to sift barley and rice and to bake bread. And he learned how to sow and harvest the seed. He not only worked very hard but did everything very cheerfully.

A year passed like this. It was the most pleasant I had spent on the island. I grew to love my man Friday. Such a good, honest man I had never known before.

As he could now speak fairly good English, I learned from him that he was of a large tribe from an island to the west of my island, the one I had seen that day from the hilltop. His tribe and another from a nearby island to the northwest were enemies, and they were often at war with one another. Both tribes would sometimes come here to eat their captives.

I learned that a tide flowed between my island and his, one way in the morning and the other way in the afternoon. A boat could just float with the tide from one place to the other. But it had to be a big boat. My canoe was much too small, Friday said.

And I learned, as I had suspected, that my island was one of the Caribbean islands off the coast of the American continent. Friday's country was the great island of Trinidad, which lay west and northwest of my island.

Having taught Friday to speak my language, my first desire was to teach him about God and about His Son, Jesus Christ. My first attempts went badly. Though Friday was quite intelligent and an excellent student, I was a poor teacher. It was then that I realized that only God can reveal Himself to a person.

I prayed constantly for wisdom. And little by little, as Friday's curiosity grew, and as he asked questions, the Lord guided me in teaching my friend about the truth of Jesus Christ. Friday easily understood the idea of Christ's dying for our sins, and he eagerly accepted the Lord as his personal Savior.

Then as I read the Bible, and as we would talk about what I read, Friday grew in knowledge and understanding. I must say that I learned as much as he did. As I attempted to teach Friday, the Lord Himself taught me through His Word, the Bible.

We spent three years like this, my best years by far on this island. With only the Word of God and God Himself to teach him, Friday became the best Christian I had ever known.

One day I learned something from Friday that gave me great hope that I might leave the island and return to England.

He told me a large boat with seventeen "bearded mans," as he put it, had come to his island a few years ago. His people had saved the men from drowning, and they lived there still.

Perhaps these were the men from the ship that had been wrecked on my island, the ship from which I had heard the gunshots. If they had gone in a boat, the current would have carried them to Friday's island.

I was curious, though, as to why Friday's people had not killed and eaten the men. I asked him.

He looked surprised at my question. "No," he said, "we make brother with them. We no eat mans but when they come to fight with us."

"What would your people do to me if I came there?" I asked.

"Me make them much love you," he said. "Friday tell them to live good, to pray to God, tell them to eat cornbread, cattleflesh, milk, no eat man again."

"Would they kill you if you told them this?"

"No, they no kill me. They much love to learn, like me."

Then Friday told me his people had already learned much from the "bearded mans."

So we decided to build a boat big enough to sail to Friday's island.

CHAPTER 16

We searched the island until we found a tree big enough and close enough to the water to make a boat for our trip. With two men now, we made our boat in about a month. Though it was big enough to carry twenty men, Friday could handle it very well on the water with his paddle.

I made a mast and sail and a rudder, for I intended to sail, not paddle. I taught Friday how to sail, and he learned quickly.

I was now in my twenty-seventh year on this island. With our boat finished, I had hope that this would be my last year here. The rainy season was upon us, and we decided we would set sail as soon as the weather cleared in November or December. But our plans were soon changed.

One day, I was busy gathering provisions for our voyage. Friday had gone to the seashore to find a turtle. Soon, back he came, running like the wind. "Master! Master!" he cried. "One, two, three canoe! There come many great number!"

He was trembling, terribly frightened that the savages had come to kill him. I placed my hand on his shoulder.

"We will fight if we must, Friday," I said. "Will you stand by me, and do as I do, and as I say?"

"Me die when you bid die, Master," he said.

Then we took fowling pieces, four muskets, and two

pistols. I wore my sword at my side. I climbed my cliff to look through the telescope. There, less than half a mile from us, were twenty cannibals preparing a feast. They had a few prisoners tied on the ground.

Friday and I crept through my handmade forest to within shooting range. I had not intended to interfere, knowing it was not my business, but God's. But when we drew nearer, I saw that one of the prisoners was not a savage, but a European. He had a long, white beard. Friday whispered that it was one of the Spaniards who had come to his island. Now two of the savages were about to club this bearded man. Then he would be cut up and roasted! *I must act now,* I thought.

"Quickly, Friday!" I said. "Do just as I do." I fired at the two savages with the Spaniard. Friday did the same. Quickly, I dropped that gun, grabbed another, and fired again. Our guns were loaded with many small bullets, which spread out in a deadly hail as we fired. With each shot two or three savages dropped.

Now we rushed forward, yelling. The cannibals were so terrified at the gunshots, they did not know which way to run. I rushed to the Spaniard and cut his bonds.

"We will talk later," I said. "We must fight now." I gave him my sword and my pistol.

Though he seemed very pale and weak, he grabbed the weapons and leapt into the fight. He fought furiously, his sword flashing.

I loaded rifles and handed them to Friday and the Spaniard, who used them faster than I could load. Friday was everywhere, hacking and hewing with his hatchet.

The few remaining savages fought back fiercely but were no match for our weapons. Soon they all lay scattered on the beach. Of the twenty who had come here, only four escaped, one of them badly wounded.

Now the Spaniard sank to the ground. I gave him water, bread, and some raisins. These refreshed him a little. He took my hand. "Señor," he said. "I will be forever in your debt for what you have done for me."

There was one prisoner tied up nearby. Friday went to cut his bonds. Then he gave a cry. Rushing forward, Friday cut the man's bonds and hugged him, crying and shouting. Then he danced in the sand, singing and weeping. "It is my father!" he cried.

This touched my heart so much that I wept, too. What a happy reunion!

But the Spaniard and Friday's father were still very weak. We made a litter and carried them to our house. There I made some stew of goat meat, barley, and rice. After resting awhile, the two men were able to tell us their story.

They had set out together in a canoe and had been captured by those other savages. They were starved for many days to weaken them, then brought here to be eaten.

Now I asked Friday if he thought that more cannibals would come to avenge those we killed. He said no. He had heard the men who escaped crying out to one another that the island was haunted by the spirits who killed by thunder and lightning (our guns), and that no one should ever come here again.

I learned that the Spaniard and his sixteen companions now on Friday's island were indeed the sailors who had been shipwrecked just off my island.

The Spaniard and Friday's father were with us for almost a year. We all laid plans for our leaving the island. It was decided that the Spaniard and Friday's father should return to their island to tell their people about me. Then, if the other Spaniards wished to, they could come back to my island, and together we could build a ship that would take us back to civilization.

So one day the two men set out, carrying a good load of supplies and well-armed with muskets and pistols.

Eight days later I saw a boat out to sea. *It must be the Spaniard,* I thought. I climbed my cliff and looked through my telescope. But it was not the boat I expected. And beyond it lay an English ship at anchor.

At first I was overjoyed at seeing the ship. But then something, some instinct, warned me. This was far out of the normal English trading routes, I knew. And there was no storm, so they were not driven here. *Perhaps they are here on some evil purpose,* I thought.

I watched them land and come ashore. There were eleven men, Englishmen by their looks. But three had their hands tied and seemed to be prisoners. The other eight wandered off, leaving the three to themselves. I watched and waited. The day wore on and the tide went out. Their boat was now aground on the beach.

When the men came back and realized they were stranded here until the tide came in, they seemed not to care. They went up the beach into the trees and lay down. Soon it seemed they were all asleep. I saw the other three some distance off in another clump of trees. I stole my way through the trees to them. Coming up behind them, I called softly. They were startled at my appearance.

"Gentlemen," I said. "Do not be surprised at me. Perhaps you may have a friend near you when you did not expect it."

One of them, with tears in his eyes, said, "Am I talking to God, or man? Are you a real man, or an angel?"

"If God had sent an angel to you, he would be better dressed than this," I said. "I am a man. I have one servant and arms and ammunition. Tell me about yourselves, and whether we may serve you."

This man told me he was the commander of that ship, and the two men with him were his officers. The crew had mutinied and taken the three men captive.

I led them to my cave. I asked the captain if he would agree to take me with him to England if I helped him get his ship back.

"Sir," he said, "I am at your command. My men and I will do anything you say, and you shall sail with us to

England if we gain back my ship. If we do not, I will be your man for the rest of my life and live or die with you wherever you go in this world."

The other two men said the same thing. I then gave them guns, and we laid plans for capturing the eight men on the island.

"Two of them are the worst," the captain said. "The others are just with them out of fear. If we can take these two, the others would gladly come back to us."

So I let the captain lead the way, as he knew the men. When we came upon them, they awoke and surrendered, all but the two leaders, who fought back and were shot dead.

Now the others begged for mercy. The captain said he would spare their lives if they swore loyalty to him and helped us capture the ship. They all swore they would.

We tied them up and left Friday to guard them in my cave until we could be sure of them. Then we sat down in my house to decide what to do next. The captain admired my home and my grove of trees. He sat shaking his head in amazement as I told him my story. And then the tears poured down his cheeks as he said that God must have put me here to deliver his ship to him.

But our battle was not yet over. There were twenty-six men still on the ship, the captain said. If this boat did not return soon, some more men would come looking for it. Would there be too many for us? How many more men might be willing to come over to us? We could only wait and hope.

CHAPTER 18

We did not have long to wait. Soon we heard a gunshot from the ship, a signal for the men on the shore to return. Of course there was no answer. Soon another shot came. Then several more.

Then, as I watched through my telescope, I saw another boat launch out from the ship and start toward shore. I counted ten men, each with a rifle. The tide came in, and the boat with it.

There were now seven of us on shore, armed and waiting. Two of our prisoners were taken into our service. They could be trusted, the captain said.

The captain watched the boat through my telescope. Three of these ten men were honest, the captain said. We should be able to win them over easily.

When the men reached the shore and found their other empty boat, they appeared confused. They called out to the men we had captured. They fired their guns. Then they gathered together, seeming to discuss what to do. After this, three of the ten got into the boat and went out a little from the shore to wait. Now the other seven came up into the woods, shooting a gun occasionally and shouting.

Now I was glad I had so carefully hidden myself here. My grove of trees was impassable, except through a certain winding path that I had cut for myself.

But we needed a plan quickly, before more men came to shore. And we decided on one.

Friday and the captain's first mate stole through the grove and down the beach a little way. There they hid, then shouted, "Hallo!"

The searching men heard this and answered. They all went off in that direction, shouting.

Friday and the first mate kept ahead of the men, shouting occasionally, and gradually led the men in a wide circle through the middle of the island. The men thought they were following the voices of their lost friends. Soon they were far away from the boat on the shore, and it was growing dark.

We waited until it was quite dark, then surprised the three on the boat. They quickly surrendered. Now, as we had planned, we met up with Friday and the first mate.

We attacked the seven men as they finally wandered up to the shore, frightened and exhausted. Two were killed, and the others surrendered. The most loyal of them eagerly came into our service. Five remained as prisoners.

Now, under cover of darkness, the captain and his crew rowed out to the ship and surprised the mutineers. There was only one shot fired, and one man killed. He was the leader of the revolt. The ship was ours!

When they came back to the shore, the captain walked up to me and bowed. "My dear friend and deliverer," he said. "There is your ship, for she is all yours, and so are we, and all that belong to her."

We embraced. And then I broke into tears and lifted my hands to heaven. I praised God, Who had delivered me as He had promised so long ago.

Before we left, I gathered some things I wanted to take with me, among them my goatskin clothes and umbrella and the gold pieces. I decided, too, that I would send a ship for the Spaniards as soon as I could.

So, on the nineteenth of December 1686, after twenty-eight years, two months, and nineteen days on this island, I boarded the ship, and we set sail for England. I had been away for thirty-five years.

THE SWISS FAMILY ROBINSON

SHIPWRECK SURVIVORS

by Johann Wyss
retold by Kristi Lorene

CHAPTER 1

For many days, the violent sea tossed us to and fro. The seamen gave up their fight and cried to God for mercy. My four young sons were horribly frightened.

"Dear children," I said, "if the Lord so wishes, He will save us from this fearful storm; if not, let us calmly put our lives in His hands and think of the joy and blessedness we will find forever in the kingdom of heaven."

We knelt to pray together. Fritz asked for the safety of his parents and younger brothers, unselfishly forgetting himself. After our brief talk with our Lord, our situation seemed somehow less frightening. A calm fell over us, and even the sea seemed to die down.

"Ah," I thought, "the Lord has heard our prayers! He will help us!"

The ship struck land with a powerful force. While much of the ship went underwater, our cabin mercifully stayed above water.

"Courage, my loved ones! Although the ship will not sail again, we will stay dry tonight. Tomorrow, if the wind and waves slow, we should be able to get ashore."

Upon those words, my children allowed themselves to enjoy the relief from the violent storm. My wife, Elizabeth, though still somewhat distressed, set about her normal duties.

"We must find some food," she said. "It will not do to go without food for long. We will need our utmost strength tomorrow."

As night fell, the storm raged once again, causing further damage to our unfortunate ship. My young ones again grew frightened.

"God will help us soon, won't He, Father?" asked Franz, my youngest son.

"You silly little boy," said Fritz. "Don't you know that we must not decide what God is to do for us? We must be patient and wait for Him."

"Well said, Fritz, had it been said kindly. You often speak harshly to your brothers, even though you may not mean to do so."

We ate a good meal, and my youngest three quickly fell to sleep. Fritz, old enough to recognize the real danger we were in, kept watch with us.

"Father, don't you think we should make swimming belts for Mother and the boys? With those they could more easily make it to shore, for you and I can swim."

His idea was such a good one that we immediately went about making them, in case of an accident during the night. My wife and young sons each put one on. After Fritz joined his brothers in sleep, my wife and I kept a prayerful watch.

At dawn I roused the boys, and we assembled on what remained of the deck. My boys were surprised to find the crew had taken the lifeboats and left us behind.

"Oh, Papa, what will we do by ourselves?" they cried.

"Children," I replied, "God will never desert us. We must trust Him. Now let us get moving."

While I and the older boys set out to find useful items, Elizabeth and young Franz went to feed the animals aboard. The poor things had been neglected for several days.

Fritz went to the arms chest, Ernest to look for tools, and Jack went to the captain's cabin. Upon opening the door, he was eagerly greeted by two large dogs who, in their excitement, toppled him head over heels. I was greatly amused to see Jack riding upon the back of the larger one when I came up the the hatchway.

We assembled in the cabin to display our treasures. Fritz had guns and plenty of bullets. Ernest had found a number of tools, including an axe, nails, and a hammer. Franz proudly showed us his box of "nice sharp little tools."

"Well done, Franz! These fishhooks will help us catch food to eat."

I praised all my boys for choosing well, then received good news from my wife that some useful animals were still alive: a cow, donkey, two goats, six sheep, a ram, and a fine pig.

We found four large barrels made of wood and bound them with iron hoops. I cut them into eight tubes and bound them together to form a sort of boat. After this, it was too late to set out for shore. We sat down to a comfortable supper, said our thankful prayers, and slept peacefully to prepare ourselves for the work of the next day.

Early the next morning, after leaving fodder within reach of the animals we had to leave behind, at least for a few days, we gathered our things and got into the little tubs, one for each of us. The elder boys took the oars, and we each wore a float belt in case we were thrown into the water.

The dogs, named Turk and Juno, left behind on the wreck, jumped into the sea to follow us. Occasionally resting their forepaws on the outriggers, they kept up with us quite well.

Bales and boxes of goods floated around us. Fritz and I got hold of a couple of hogsheads, or large barrels, and towed them alongside.

The dogs scrambled to shore before us and greeted us with delighted barking. The flamingos on shore added to the din of the geese and ducks we'd brought along. I was glad for the noise, thinking of all the dinners these birds would furnish.

We gathered our children around us on dry land and knelt to offer thanks for our safety. We then gave ourselves to God's keeping.

After unloading, I set about arranging a fireplace out of large flat stones, while the boys collected moss and grass to spread in the tent for our beds.

Fritz, leaving a gun with me and taking another with him, went to see what lay beyond the stream. While trying to lift two casks from alongside our boat, I heard Jack shouting for help. Hatchet in hand, I went and found him standing in a deep pool where a huge lobster had caught his leg in its powerful claw. I freed him, and Jack, proud of his capture, took it to his mother and wanted her to make lobster soup right away.

"Please," she laughed, "I prefer to cook one new dish at a time!"

Ernest also told of finding something good to eat—oysters. I told him to fetch a few for our next meal.

Shortly after supper, night fell on our first day on shore. We loaded our guns for protection and offered prayers to God. We thanked Him for His mercy, gave ourselves to His care, and, as the last ray of light departed, closed our tent and lay down to sleep.

In the morning, Fritz and I each took a gun and game bag, and Fritz stuck a pair of pistols in his belt, and I a small hatchet. Breakfast over, and the youngsters convinced our expeditions too dangerous for them, we stowed away some biscuits and water and were ready to set off exploring our island.

"Stop!" I exclaimed. "We have forgotten something very important. We have not yet joined in morning prayer. Amid the cares and pleasures of this life, we often forget the God to Whom we owe all things."

After we were within God's protective care, Fritz and I set off, a little fearful of what might happen to us in this unknown place. We were not sure whether we would find our ship companions, who had left us to fend for ourselves.

Alas, we did not find our shipmates. We did, however, find some gourds that we split for use as plates and bowls.

Turk had followed us, and when we came to a thicket of reeds, I sent him ahead in fear that we'd come upon a venomous snake. I cut one of the reeds, intending to use it as a weapon against snakes, and noticed thick juice coming from one end. I tasted it and found it quite sweet. Sugarcane! Fritz grew quite excited and cut a dozen and carried them in a bundle under his arm.

During our homeward journey, Turk, quite hungry, jumped upon a mother monkey carrying her baby on her back. Fritz plunged in too late to save her, and the young monkey jumped onto his back, holding fast to his thick, curly hair.

Fritz begged to keep the little creature. "Very well," I agreed. "But you must train him carefully; otherwise, his natural instincts will prove mischievous instead of useful to us."

Juno was the first to notice our arrival home and gave a loud bark, to which Turk replied. A tumult of excited voices rose when my youngsters noticed the furry creature clinging to their oldest brother. I had to wait a few moments for their excitement to die down a little, so my wife could hear when I spoke to her.

"I am thankful to God to find you all well and safe. Our expedition went well, though we found no trace of our shipmates."

"If it be the will of God," she said, "that we dwell alone on this island, let us be content and thankful we are all safe."

CHAPTER 2

We decided to revisit the wreck while it was still calm, to save the animals we had left there and bring to land any items that would be useful to us. We had built ourselves a sort of boat for this purpose.

Before Fritz and I departed, I erected a signal post and hoisted a strip of sailcloth as a flag. I told Elizabeth the flag should remain hoisted as long as all was well on shore.

"Should you need us to return, fire three shots and lower the flag."

"Very well. Now let us kneel and ask a blessing before you and Fritz depart."

The animals aboard the wreck greeted us with great joy. They were not hungry, for we had left them well supplied, but seemed delighted by the mere sight of human beings.

We had so much to do aboard the wreck, I signalled to my wife that we'd be staying the night. Our ship had sailed for the purpose of supplying a young colony. We gathered quantities of weapons and ammunition. We then went to the kitchen and took stock of knives, forks, and kitchen utensils. In the captain's cabin, we even discovered a service of silver tableware.

We supplied ourselves with potted meats, soups, hams, sausages, a bag of maize and wheat, and a supply of seeds and vegetables. I added a barrel of sulphur for use in making matches. Nails, tools, and farming implements added to our cargo and sank our handmade boat so low I would have had to lighten her if the sea had been choppy.

As night came on, we exchanged signals with those on shore to assure each other of our safety. Fritz and I knelt with a prayer for the safety of our dear ones on shore. Fritz was soon sound asleep, but the thought of my wife and youngsters on shore, alone and unprotected, disturbed my rest.

The next day, we devised a plan to bring the animals ashore.

"Father," said Fritz, "perhaps we could make swimming belts, as we did for Mother and the children."

With the animals in their swimming belts, after some great struggle, we steered for shore, drawing our herd behind us. I took up my glass and tried to see how my dear ones were faring on shore, when I was startled by a shout. I glanced up to see Fritz standing, his gun aimed at a shark who was thinking one of our sheep would make him a nice dinner. When the shark turned on his side to seize his prey, and his white belly appeared, Fritz fired, and I watched a trace of blood form on the calm water.

"Well done, Fritz!"

On shore, we gleefully greeted our loved ones and unloaded our cargo.

Our supper that night was quite different from our first on this island.

My wife had made a table out of a board placed atop two casks; on this was a white tablecloth, along with the knives, forks, spoons, and plates Fritz and I found.

Over a feast of soup, ham, cheese, biscuits, and butter, we each related our adventures.

My wife wove a splendid tale of a trip through the woods. She told of a grove of trees she had discovered, and her desire to live high up in one, among the leaves.

"Now," she said, completing her tale, "I hope that tomorrow you will do me the favor of packing up and taking me to live among my splendid trees."

"So, little wife," I grinned, "that is your idea of comfort and security? A tree, of unknown height, on which we perch and roost like birds? If we had wings or balloons, it might indeed be a good plan."

"Laugh if you will, but we would be safe from the jackals and other creatures of the night. And I have seen such a home in our beloved Switzerland. It was in a pretty arbor, with a strong floor, up in the branches of a tree. We went up a staircase to reach it. Why could we not build a place like that, where we could sleep safely at night?"

I pondered this a moment. "I will consider the idea; perhaps something will come of it after all! But our supper is now over, and night is coming on. Let us commend ourselves to the Almighty's protection and go to bed."

My wife was a bit distressed when I told her a bridge would have to be built before we could move to her beloved trees. "I shall be parched to death by the heat in these rocks, if a bridge must be built before we leave! Can't we walk across with things on our backs, as we did before? The cow and donkey could carry a great deal."

"They could. But we still need bags and baskets to carry things in. We still need a bridge, which I will start on right away while you work on the baskets."

The children were overjoyed when told of our proposed move. They talked of it as our journey to the Promised Land.

Ernest and Fritz accompanied me to the wreck, where we obtained planks for making the bridge. Having no surveyor's table to help us determine if our planks were long enough to reach across, we had to heed Ernest's advice.

"How about a ball of string, Father? Tie one end to a stone, throw it across, then draw it back and measure the line!"

Using this, we judged the distance across at eighteen feet. Then, allowing three extra feet on each end, I calculated twenty-four feet as the necessary length of the boards.

During dinner, my wife showed me two large canvas bags she had made.

We quickly ate and returned to complete our bridge. When our work was done, we were all severely tired, and we gratefully fell into our beds.

After breakfast the next morning, we all fluttered around in activity. Some collected food, others packed kitchen utensils, ropes, and hammocks and loaded them onto the cow and donkey. My wife insisted on taking the poultry, so away ran the children to catch the cocks and hens, until the mother called her panting and unsuccessful boys back. Only by scattering grain were we able to gather the fowls.

We filled the tent with things we would return for later and secured it with chests and casks placed around it.

During our journey, the dogs had an unfortunate encounter with a large porcupine. Little Jack pulled a pistol from his pocket and shot it dead. After much effort, he proudly dragged the creature and presented it to his mother.

"Please, Father, let us take it," Jack pleaded, while his mother pulled five or six quills from each dog. "He is good to eat."

We made a somewhat awkward bundle of the porcupine and resumed our march. The beautiful appearance of the trees was exactly as my wife had described. I knew right away, if an abode could be made among the branches, it would be the safest, most charming home in the world.

We unloaded the animals, set the poultry at their liberty, then sat down to rest and make our plans for the night.

Ernest found flat stones to make a fireplace, while Franz gathered sticks. Their mother, of course, was anxious to cook food.

Just as Ernest and I were discussing what kind of trees we were camping under, little Franz came running with a large bundle of sticks and his mouth full.

"Oh, Mother," he cried, "this is so delicious!"

His mother quickly made him empty his mouth. "Don't swallow it! It is very likely poisonous!"

I assured my wife the figs he found were quite harmless.

"But remember, Franz," I scolded, "you must never eat any-thing without first showing me, no matter how good it seems."

Knips, our monkey friend, was given a fig. He turned it about, sniffing and smelling, then popped it into his mouth and remained unharmed.

We examined all the trees and finally chose one that would be our home. The branches spread high above us. My plan was to make a rope ladder if we could succeed in getting a string tossed across a strong bough.

With dinner over that evening, I prepared temporary sleeping quarters for the night. By using hammocks to form an arched roof among the branches, then covering the rest with sailcloth, we made a temporary shelter.

While my wife made a harness for the animals, for use in their drawing beams up to our tree, I walked down to the beach with Fritz and Ernest to search for wood for building our new home. I also hoped to find some lightweight rods to form a ladder.

For a time, we found only rough driftwood, which we could not use.

Then Ernest pointed to bamboo, half-buried in the sand. I stripped off the leaves and cut them to a length of five feet each. After I put them in bundles, I began to look for small reeds to use as arrows.

We returned to our loved ones, where I got a ball of string from my wife. I tied one end of the string to one of my arrows, took up my newly made bow, and aimed at a large branch above me. The arrow took the thread over the branch and fell at our feet. Exactly as I wanted! Now for the rope ladder.

The boys, who watched intently while I made the ladder, were each eager to be first.

"Jack shall have the honor," I said, "as he is the lightest. Up with you, my boy, and don't break your neck!"

Jack hurried up the ladder to the top, where he waved his cap. "Three cheers for the nest! What a grand house we shall have up here! Come along, Fritz!"

Fritz scrambled up with a hammer and nails and fastened the ladder more securely. I followed with an axe and surveyed the tree. It would nicely suit us.

My wife fastened a pulley to a cord hanging beside the ladder. I pulled it up and fastened it to a stout branch above me so that we could use it to haul up the beams we would need tomorrow. Finding the boys in my way, I sent them down. I worked by the light of the moon until I was quite worn out, then descended to have supper.

After feasting on roast shoulder of porcupine, soup, cheese, butter, and biscuits, we called our cattle and fowl. We built a glorious fire to keep off prowling beasts and lay down to rest.

I found it hard to sleep. As soon as one thought was pushed away, another came in. I replenished the fire and only fell asleep in my hammock toward morning.

In the morning, my wife milked the goats and cow while we fed the animals and went to the beach to collect more wood for our house. The large beams we harnessed to the cow and donkey, while we dragged the others.

Fritz and I enclosed our house on two sides, for the great trunk provided a third wall. We left the front open to admit the fresh sea breeze and used sailcloth for a roof. We then came down and built a table and benches from the remaining wood. After working like slaves all day, Fritz and I flung ourselves on the grass while my wife arranged supper on her new table.

After supper, we lit our watchfires and climbed up to our new home. My boys eagerly climbed up, but my wife went cautiously, unsure of being at such a height from the ground.

For the first time, we all stood together in our new home. I drew up the ladder, and with greater security than since we'd landed on the island, offered up our evening prayer and retired for the night.

CHAPTER 3

The children woke the next morning, eager and springing about like young monkeys.

"What shall we do today?"

"Rest."

"Rest?" they replied.

"Six days thou shalt labor, but on the seventh thou shalt rest."

"Oh, jolly," said Jack. "I shall take a bow and arrow and shoot. We'll climb about the tree and have fun all day."

"That is not how you will spend the Lord's Day," I said.

"But we can't go to church here."

"The shade of this tree is far more beautiful than any church. Here we will worship our creator." One by one the children slipped down the ladder. I took my wife aside.

"My dear Elizabeth," I said. "This morning we will devote to the Lord. But it will be impossible to keep them quiet the whole day. After services, I will allow them innocent recreation, then in the evening we will take a walk."

During our evening meal, I spoke about naming the different spots we had visited on this coast. We began by naming the bay in which we landed Safety Bay. Our first home we called Tentholm; the islet in the bay, Shark Island; and the reedy swamp, Flamingo Marsh. After some time we named our tree home Falconhurst.

Following our evening walk, we closed our Sabbath day with a prayer and glad hymn of praise. We slept with our hearts full of peace.

The next day, while the boys and I were out exploring, Ernest sped toward me, bearing a plant in his hand.

"Potatoes! Father, potatoes!"

"Yes," Jack chimed in, "acres and acres of potatoes!"

"Ernest, you have indeed made a great discovery. With potatoes we shall never starve!"

We filled our pockets and pouches with potatoes. That night, we had a delicious supper of potatoes, milk, and butter.

One evening, we found a great deal of driftwood on the sand. I planned to use it to build a sledge, to make fetching our stores at Tentholm much easier.

I roused Ernest to assist me, hoping to cure his laziness. After much yawning and stretching, he did seem pleased to go on an expedition with me while the others slept.

"I suppose," I said to him, "that you feel sorry for yourself for having to leave your cozy bed so early."

"Oh, Father," he laughed. "Pray, do not laugh at my laziness. With the grace of God, I intend to cure myself of it."

Our work on shore was quickly completed. We selected the wood fit for making a sledge and, with the help of our donkey, dragged it homeward. We also towed along a small chest that I'd found buried in the sand. The chest, which had belonged to a common sailor, contained only his clothes, now soaked with sea water.

The boys were practicing their shooting on an array of birds when Ernest and I returned. In the interest of saving gunpowder, I suggested they make snares to trap the birds. The younger ones did so, while Fritz and Ernest helped me build the sledge.

Though my sons didn't mind making the snares, they were disturbed by the order to use our ammunition sparingly.

"Papa," little Franz said, "couldn't we just plant more gunpowder right away?"

My older boys burst into laughter. I, too, found it difficult to keep a serious face.

"All right, Boys," I said. "We have had our amusement, now tell your brother what gunpowder really is."

"It's not grown from seeds," Ernest explained. "It's a mixture of charcoal, sulphur, and saltpeter."

I turned my full attention to finishing the sledge. When I finally looked up from my work, I saw that my wife and sons were preparing to roast about two dozen wild birds. For a spit, Elizabeth had used a long narrow sword blade that had belonged to one of the ship's officers.

"Liz," I said, "isn't it a bit wasteful to cook them all at once?"

She smiled slyly. "After dinner, you can test your new sledge by fetching me a butter cask. I can preserve the half-cooked birds in butter."

After dinner, Ernest went with me to fetch the cask, and

later, I sent him to collect salt needed at home. When he had left I went to bathe.

Feeling greatly refreshed, I returned to the spot only to find my son not there.

"Father, Father!" I heard him call. "I've caught a large fish! So large, he drags the line!"

I headed toward his voice and found him lying on the grass, trying to hold on to a rod.

I took the rod from him, gave the fish more line, and slowly led it into shallow water. Ernest ran in and killed it with his hatchet. It was a salmon of, I guessed, around fifteen pounds.

"Wonderful, Ernest! Think how delighted your mother will be when we bring this beauty home."

While Ernest bathed, I cleaned and packed the salmon for our journey home. Later we harnessed our beasts to the well-laden sledge and returned home.

We were on the borders of a thicket when Juno, who had tagged along, plunged into the bushes, barking fiercely. A creature, taking flying leaps in a sitting posture, covered the ground at an astonishing rate. I tried to shoot it as it passed, but missed. Ernest, behind me, watched coolly. His eyes seemed to mark a spot. He fired and shot the creature dead.

We were surprised by this creature. As large as a sheep, its head and skin color were like that of a mouse. Further, it had the long ears of a hare, and the tail of a tiger. The forepaws were small as a squirrel's, but the hind legs were enormous.

"It has four sharp incisor teeth, Father," Ernest said. "Two upper and two lower."

"Then it is a rodent."

We assumed it to be a kangaroo of sorts and added it to the already heavy load.

We arrived late at Falconhurst and hastily went to work preparing the kangaroo, part for immediate use and part for future salting.

After a hearty supper of broiled salmon and potatoes, we then gave great thanks to our Lord and retired to our well-earned bed.

Fritz and I returned to the wreck, where we used old water casks and planks to build a raft. After a supper from the ship's provisions, we rested on the wreck for the night.

Next morning, we loaded the raft and our boat, first carrying off the contents of our own cabins. From the captain's room we took the furniture, door, and window frames, along with their bolts, bars, and locks. We next took chests belonging to the officers, carpenter, and gunsmith.

One chest was filled with an assortment of gold and silver watches, snuffboxes, buckles, studs, chains, rings, and other trinkets. We also found a box of money and a case of common knives and forks, more suited to us than the fancy silver ones we had already taken ashore.

We also found carefully packed fruit trees, along with plumbers' tools, lead, paint, farming implements, and sacks of maize, peas, oats, and wheat.

Bewildered by the wealth around us, we had to carefully choose what we would take. We could not take it all, and the next storm would most likely destroy what remained of the ship. We selected the most useful articles, and, early in the afternoon, our crafts were both laden.

Partway through our journey back to Tentholm, Fritz shot a harpoon with a rope tied to the end into the shell of a giant turtle. The turtle towed us to shore where my wife made plans to cook it. Fritz decided its shell would make a useful water trough.

With all of us pitching in to unload our treasures, we lost no time in making the trip back to Falconhurst. The calm sea and fine weather tempted me, a few days later, to make another trip to the wreck. We collected a copper boiler pot, iron plates, tobacco grates, two grindstones, a small barrel of powder, a barrel of lints, and two wheelbarrows.

On shore, I found my wife had exerted herself to provide a good store of potatoes and manioc root, with which we could have also sown seeds for Indian corn, melons, pumpkins, and cucumbers each time she went for potatoes.

"Tell me, Elizabeth, where do these seeds come from?"

"Out of my magic bag, of course," she replied, patting the bag she had not departed from since leaving the wreck.

Her eyes then rested on the tobacco graters.

"Make your mind easy, Wife. I do not intend to make snuff. These will help in making bread."

"But we have not an oven."

"Ah, you mustn't expect real loaves. In these flat irons I can bake flat cakes, or scones."

Spreading a piece of sailcloth on the ground, I summoned my boys to grate their supply of well-washed manioc root. No one was tempted to stop and taste the flour, for it looked like wet sawdust.

"What is the good of pressing this, Father?" asked Ernest.

I explained we had to extract the sap, which was poisonous, and use only the wholesome and nourishing dry pith. But, of course, I would first try the effect of the cakes on the fowls and monkey.

We filled a canvas bag Elizabeth had made with the damp powder and squeezed all moisture from it. I made only one cake that day and fed it to Knips and the fowls. The morning found them lively and healthy, and we eagerly set about to make more for our own use.

Now that I had learned how to provide my family with bread, my thoughts fell to the valuables still within the wreck. I coaxed Elizabeth into letting me take all the boys with me, except little Franz.

"But you must promise," she added, "that you will not spend a night on board. It's not safe."

"Yes, Liz."

Once aboard the wreck, I told the boys to collect whatever first came to hand.

"I want the raft loaded in time for our return home."

I sent the boys away to amuse themselves with whatever

they could find, while I tried to figure out a way to gain possession of a small pinnace, or ship's boat, that lay in pieces on the wreck.

The beautiful little vessel lay wedged in a narrow space, making it impossible to put together there. The parts were so heavy that taking them piece by piece to another location seemed equally impossible.

My eyes grew accustomed to the dim light that filtered into the small compartment. I noticed each part of the pinnace was carefully arranged and numbered. If I only had space to work in, the craft would certainly float and be of great use to us in the future, both as a work craft and one for pleasure craft.

"Boys!" I cried, as they returned to see what I was up to. "Fetch axes. Break down this compartment and clear a space all around."

We worked until evening drew near and had barely made a dent in the mass of woodwork. A lot of work and perseverance lay ahead of us before we could call ourselves the owner of this useful and elegant little boat.

We landed ashore, feeling too tired to walk to Falconhurst. To our pleasure, Elizabeth and Franz were waiting at Tentholm for us.

"I thought it best to take up quarters here, while you're working on the wreck."

"A grand idea, my good and sensible wife! I promise we will work hard, so that you may return soon to your beloved Falconhurst."

"Mother," said Fritz. "Come see what we've brought for you to add to your stores."

The boys proudly presented their mother with two small casks of butter, three of flour, corn, rice, and a number of articles welcomed by any careful housewife.

We worked many days on the pinnace. At length, with incredible labor, it was finished. She stood ready to be launched, yet imprisoned in the wreck's massive wooden walls that defied our strength.

I could think of no way to free her. I was near despair when an idea came to me. If I could carry out the plan, the pinnace would be released without further delay or labor.

I got a large cast-iron mortar, filled it with gun powder, and secured a block of oak on the top. I then pierced a hole through the oak for the insertion of a match. Thus, when the mortar exploded, it would blow out the side of the wreck next to the pinnace.

Without telling the boys my plan, and with my heart beating rapidly, I told them to get into the boat. I lit the match I had prepared, which would burn awhile before reaching the powder, and we made for land.

As we were unloading the raft ashore, my anxiety was not noticed as I waited and listened. Then—a flash! a mighty roar! a grand plume of smoke!

My terror-stricken family all turned their eyes toward the sea.

"Perhaps you left a fire burning too near the gun

powder," my wife said.

"Perhaps," I quietly replied. "I shall go see. Will anyone come along?"

The boys sprang into the boat while I whispered reassurances to my wife. We pulled for the wreck faster than we ever had before.

My plan had worked! The pinnace was in full view! The boys gazed at me for a moment, then guessed my secret.

"You planned it, you clever father!"

We secured our prize at a sheltered spot and returned to Tentholm. We spent several days completing the rigging and adding two brass guns.

My wife had not been told of the pinnace. The day we sailed her home, my boys fired a salute as we neared shore. We brought the pinnace near the bank, and Fritz helped Elizabeth on board.

"You dear, horrid, wonderful men!" she exclaimed. "I don't know whether to scold you or praise you!"

After the pinnace was shown off, my wife had a surprise of her own.

"You must come and see how little Franz and I have used our time in your absence."

We found a garden neatly laid out in beds and walks.

"My dear, it is beautiful work!"

"The ground was light and easy to dig."

She and Franz had planted potatoes and cassava roots. There was space for sugarcane and young fruit trees.

"You will need to irrigate them," she said, "by leading water from the cascades in hollow bamboo shoots."

She spent the rest of the evening explaining her plan to have pineapples, melons, European vegetables, and maize.

CHAPTER 4

We passed many Sundays at Tentholm, so we could easily reach the wreck to gather supplies to take with us to Falconhurst. We had undergone great heat and hard work and welcomed yet another day of rest, to be observed with heartfelt devotion and praise.

In the evening, I asked the boys to let me see them in athletic exercises: running, leaping, wrestling, and climbing.

"I want to see my sons strong, both morally and physically; brave to do what is good and right, to hate evil, and strong to work hard and provide for themselves and others and to fight if necessary."

The following day, I took a long cord and fastened a lead bullet to each end. The boys, naturally, were curious as to what I was doing.

"This is a miniature lasso." I then used a tree stump to show them how to use the lasso. Cheering my skill, they each asked for a lasso of their own.

While making the trip back to Falconhurst, I found a bush with wax suitable for making candles. Fritz made a discovery of his own, in a gummy resin coming from a tree.

"Oh, Father, look! This gum is quite elastic. Can it be India rubber?"

"What!" I cried. "A valuable discovery that would be."

It was, indeed, India rubber, I was quite excited, for it could be used to make boots and shoes, as well as bottles and bowls.

The boys were quite anxious to learn to make candles. Though I didn't tell them, I was not certain how this venture would turn out. We had the wax but no animal fat, which is needed to make candles burn longer and brighter. In spite of my misgivings, we set to work.

We picked berries and put them in a pot over a fire. The green was added and melted, rising to the surface of the juice made from the cooking berries. This we skimmed off and put in a separate pot, repeating this several times until we had enough liquid wax for our use.

I then took the wicks my wife had prepared and dipped them into the wax, several times, until they were thick and sturdy. Fritz hung them on a bush to dry. That night, we were able to stay up three hours after sunset, like civilized human beings, and Falconhurst was for the first time brightly lit.

After planting our fruit trees in such a manner that they formed a shady avenue along Falconhurst, we laid down a crude road, making it possible to reach Tentholm even if the weather was bad.

We then turned all our attention to Tentholm. It did not have to be as beautiful as Falconhurst, but it did have to be a safe place of refuge in case of emergency. I planted a thick, prickly hedge to protect us from wild animals, made the bridge stronger, and mounted a couple of guns on two small hills.

Six weeks of hard labor went by. I saw this hard work was developing the boys' strength. I once again encouraged them to practice running, leaping, climbing, and swimming.

I also noticed their clothing, despite their mother's mending and patching, was looking untidy. I was determined to make another visit to the wreck, to replenish our wardrobe and see how much longer the ship was likely to hold together. I took three of the boys with me.

"Come, boys, not an article of any value must be left on board. Rummage her out to the very bottom of her hold."

A sailor's chest, cloth and linen, small guns, a table, benches, windows, shutters, bolts and locks, and barrels of pitch were soon heaped on deck. We loaded the raft and went to shore, returning to the wreck with our boat in tow. After a few more trips, nothing was left on board. I told my wife, before our final trip, that two barrels of gunpowder were intentionally left on board.

"I'm going to blow her up."

We knew her destruction was for the best. Yet that night we went to bed sad, as if we had lost a dear old friend.

Late one evening while we enjoyed our dinner, our donkey, Grizzle, lay drowsing. Suddenly, he brayed loudly, pricked up his ears, kicked up his heels, and galloped into a thicket of bamboo. I sent the dogs in chase, but they returned without the donkey. Because it was quite late, we had to abandon our search.

This incident alarmed me. We had lost Grizzle, and I didn't

know what had caused his sudden flight. Perhaps by instinct he sensed the approach of some wild beast. I built a large fire and told my family to sleep with their firearms by their sides.

Next morning after breakfast, we went to search for Grizzle. We followed his tracks until he mingled with a herd of some larger animals. I nearly turned back, but Jack urged us on.

"Father, if we can make it to a hill, we will certainly be able to see such a large herd at a distance."

I decided to detour through a bamboo marsh. The bamboo were huge, with some plants over thirty feet high. Suddenly, we found ourselves face-to-face with the herd we sought—a herd of buffaloes! Jack would have fired had I not stopped him.

"No, Jack! Back to the thicket and keep the dogs back!"

Despite our efforts to restrain them, the dogs dashed in and grabbed a buffalo calf. The elder buffaloes bellowed loudly, pawed the ground and tore at it with their horns, then dashed toward us. We scarcely had time to get behind a rock before the leader was upon us. I drew my pistol and shot him dead. The others stopped, sniffed the air, then turned and galloped across the plain.

The dogs still struggled with the calf but could not bring it down. I didn't want to shoot, for if we could tame the creature we would have a fine beast of burden.

Jack lassoed the calf to the ground. We called off the dogs, and the animal was at our mercy.

"Now what will we do with him?" asked Jack, looking at

the beast panting on the ground.

"I'll show you."

I fastened its legs together and, while Jack held the calf's head, pierced the cartilage of the calf's nose with my knife. When the blood flow slowed, I passed a heavy cord through the hole.

I didn't relish paining the animal, but it was a necessity. We set the calf on his legs, and, subdued, he followed us without resistance.

I turned to the dead buffalo. I cut out its tongue and a couple of steaks, then packed them in salt, and left the rest to the dogs.

Back home, I calculated the number of animals and pets we had acquired since landing here. The boys agreed that each would look after his own animal. We gave our praise to God for our safe return and ate a delicious supper.

CHAPTER 5

The boys and I went out one morning to our avenue of trees. We found many had fallen and others were bent. We tied them up again with bamboo.

As we digested our dinner later that day, my wife asked if I could make a flight of steps to reach Falconhurst.

"I should like to be able to get to our lovely nest without having to scale that ladder!" she said.

I told her a staircase outside would be impossible. "But inside, perhaps. I have thought this trunk may be hollow."

In their eagerness to prove the trunk was hollow, the boys were soon climbing, peeping into, and tapping on the trunk. They disturbed a nest of bees and were promptly attacked. Jack fared the worst, and his face had to be treated with cold earth to ease the pain.

I wanted to keep some of the bees, so I made a hive for them out of a large gourd. I added a straw roof as protection from rain and heat.

That night we filled every hole in the trunk with wet clay. Next morning, I took a hollow cane and put one end through the clay and into the tree. I then pumped in smoke until the intense buzzing in the trunk stopped; the bees were stupefied.

Fritz and I carefully cut a small door in the trunk. The bees hung there in clusters, and we placed them in the hive. I then took their wax and honey from their storehouses and put it in a cask.

Come evening, we separated the honey from the honey-comb and poured it into jars and pots. The rest we boiled until it was fluid. Then we placed it in a canvas bag and squeezed out all the honey. We saved the remaining wax for candlemaking.

Next morning, we set to building Mother her staircase. We first cut a hinged door, then cleared rotten wood from the center of the tree. We formed the steps with planks that had washed on shore from the blown-up wreck and secured them in place with nails. Upward we built, cutting windows to allow air and light, until we were even with the center pole. We continued around and around until we reached the floor to Falconhurst. It took us a month to build the staircase.

I then turned to the task of shoemaker. With India rubber for the uppers, and a strip of buffalo hide for the soles, I had a pair of comfortable, durable, nice-looking waterproof boots. Orders poured in from all sides, and soon the whole family was likewise provided for.

Our animal kingdom grew. Grizzle, our donkey, which had disappeared for a few days, returned with a companion, an onager or wild donkey. We had our dogs, bees, geese, and three broods of chickens that had hatched. Reminded of the approaching rainy season, I set about making shelter for these animals.

We first made a roof over the roots of our tree, using

bamboo canes for the framework. We then used clay and moss over the top and coated the hole with a mixture of tar and lime water to keep out rain. When we were finished, the stables, poultry yard, and dining hall were all under one roof. Our winter quarters now established, we had only to fill them with food. We collected potatoes, grouse, eggs, and acorns.

Franz discovered some great "swords," as he called them, which turned out to be leaves of New Zealand flax. I knew their value and could not rest until I had shared this discovery with Elizabeth.

"Oh, what a delightful find!" she exclaimed. "No one shall be clothed in rags! Just make me a spindle, and you shall have shirts and stockings and trousers!"

While Elizabeth set about her tailoring, we continued gathering food for the winter: potatoes, manioc, coconuts, sweet acorns, and sugarcane. Our corn was sowed, our animals housed, and our food stored when down came the rain.

Our treetop dwelling was crowded. We carried in our furniture, so it would not be harmed by rain. The animals and provisions were below us, and our beds and household goods hemmed us in on every side.

Although we kept ourselves busy, time dragged by. Our mornings were occupied tending the animals. The boys assisted me in making carding combs and a spindle for their mother.

In the evening, by the candlelight, I wrote a journal of all the events that had happened since our arrival on this land.

Mother was busy with her needle, Ernest sketched birds, beasts, and flowers he had met during the past few months, and Fritz and Jack taught little Franz to read.

Weeks went by. Week after week we were close prisoners. Rain pounded down above us. Constant gloom hung over the desolate scene.

CHAPTER 6

The rain finally ceased; spring had come. We stepped out of our winter abode, joyful as freed prisoners.

The seeds we had sown were shooting through the damp earth. Everything around us looked refreshed.

I wanted to visit Tentholm to see how our stores had fared. Fritz and I went together and found our tent blown to the ground, the canvas torn to rags, our provisions soaked, and two casks of powder destroyed. We spread a few things out to dry and decided we should find a safer place before next winter. Fritz proposed we hollow out a cave in the rock.

The rock we chose turned out to be a salt cavern. We returned to Falconhurst, our minds full of plans for turning our new discovery to the best possible advantage.

We talked of nothing but the new house, of how it should be filled up. We decided to keep up Falconhurst as a summer residence. Our cave would be formed into a winter house.

We cut a row of windows in the rock and fitted them with window cases we had brought from the officers' cabins. We brought the door from Falconhurst and fitted it, too.

We divided the cave into four parts: In front we had our sitting, eating, and sleeping rooms; on the right was our kitchen and workshop; on the left, our stables. In the back was our storehouse. We built a proper fireplace and chimney.

One morning as we approached Tentholm, I noticed a disturbance in the water. A bank of herrings was making for shore.

We soon had a fishery in operation. Jack and Fritz captured them, while we on shore cleaned them and placed them in casks: first a layer of salt, then a layer of herrings, and so on until we had filled and rolled many casks to our storehouse.

Our good fortune did not end there. A great number of seals appeared on shore, attracted by the herring scraps we had thrown into the sea. Though not suitable for our stable, their skins would be useful in harnesses and clothing, and their fat we boiled down to oil for use in tanning, soap making, and burning in lamps.

This wonderful climate did well for our garden. Peas, beans, wheat, barley, rye, and Indian corn were always ripe, as well as cucumbers, melons, and assorted vegetables. I hoped my experiment at Falconhurst was doing as well and set out one morning to see.

We found the former potato fields covered with barley, wheat, rye, and peas. I was amazed. Elizabeth and Franz had, in my absence during trips to the wreck, scattered the seeds. I congratulated my wife and youngest son.

I wanted to have a somewhat civilized farm a distance from Falconhurst, where we could place some of our animals. We harnessed the buffalo, cow, and donkey to the cart and loaded it with a dozen fowls, four young pigs, two couples of pigs, two couples of goats, and a pair of hens and one cock grouse. We made a path through the woods and tall grasses toward Cape Disappointment.

We found a large field covered with white flakes that Franz mistook for snow. "Oh, Mother, come down from the cart and play snowballs," he called.

We surmised the plants in the field were dwarf cotton trees. Mother was charmed by this delightful discovery. We gathered a great quantity of cotton into three bags and resumed our journey.

We finally decided on a pretty wooded hill for our farm. There were shade trees, thick grass, and even a sparkling brook. Here there would be a pasture, water, shade, and shelter.

Fritz and I found a group of trees that would serve as posts for a shed. We carried our tools to the spot and had just enough time for supper. Afterward, we lay down on the beds Elizabeth had prepared for us with the cotton.

The next day we spent building our shed. While gathering up scraps of bark for our fire, I noticed a peculiar smell. Some of the pieces of bark were from the terebinth tree, others from the American fir.

"From the fir," I said, "we get turpentine and tar. We can make pitch for our yacht with tar and oil. And cart grease, too, with tar and fat."

It took several days to build our farmhouse, which we divided into three parts: one for stalls for the animals, one with perches for the birds, and a third furnished with rough tables and benches to serve as sleeping quarters for us when we found it necessary to stay at the farm site.

We left an ample supply of food for the animals and, after naming our farm Woodlands, set out again.

We found a beautiful hill and decided to make a cottage there, so that the lovely spot might be visited occasionally. In only a few days, the rustic abode was completed, and Ernest named the place Prospect Hill.

During this expedition, I had hoped to find some trees from whose bark I could make a canoe. I finally came upon two tall, straight trees, something like birch, that would do nicely.

I did all the work I could without a wide variety of tools, then sent Fritz and Jack to get the sledge—which now ran on wheels taken from gun carriages aboard the wreck. With the sledge, the canoe could be taken to the harbor at Tentholm and completed.

It was time to rest for the night when they returned, but early dawn found us busy again, eager to complete our canoe and return to Tentholm. However, quite worn out, we stopped for the night at Falconhurst before taking the canoe to the harbor at Tentholm.

I was very proud of my canoe and had even added my own touch: Two large, airtight bags made from the skin of dogfish were fastened on each side, just above water level. These floats would prevent the canoe from sinking or tipping over, no matter how loaded down she was.

Our animal kingdom had gained three new members: a

bull calf that Franz had named Grumble and Juno's two pups named Bruno and Fang.

We worked for two months at the salt cave to finish it before the rainy season. We even took a large piece of sail-cloth, saturated it with a strong liquid made of glue and isinglass, and laid wool and hair from the sheep and goats on it. When dried, this made a grand carpet for the floor of our sitting room.

One morning I woke early, with my thoughts considering how long we had been on this coast. To my surprise, I found that the next day would mark one year. My heart swelled with thankfulness to God, Who had made us safe then loaded us with so many useful things on this island. I resolved to set the next day as a day of Thanksgiving. At supper, I told my family of the coming event.

"Good people, do you know that tomorrow is a very great and important day? We shall use that day to honor our merciful escape to this land and call it Thanksgiving Day."

For the special day, I wanted my children to remember the storm of a year ago so they would have a deep sense of gratitude for our escape from death. I read aloud passages from my journal, as well as many beautiful verses from the Psalms. We were all led to bless and praise the name of the Lord our deliverer.

After our Thanksgiving dinner, I announced a "Grand Display of Athletic Sports" for the afternoon.

"Your mother and I will be the spectators and judges."

The boys thought this a grand idea. They asked about events and, of course, prizes.

"The judges will award prizes in shooting, running, riding, leaping, climbing, and swimming."

The children bustled about making preparations. All this activity sent the ducks and geese gaggling and quacking in fright. The effect was absurd and had the boys greatly amused.

"We will have shooting first," I said, "and the other activities will come later, when it is cooler."

I took a board and roughly shaped it like a kangaroo. Jack was not happy until he had added ears and a long leather strap for a tail.

Each boy fired twice. Fritz hit the head both times. Ernest hit the body once and missed his second shot. Jack shot the ears clean off the head.

I then had them load their pistols with a small shot and threw a little board as high in the air as I could.

"You must aim and hit it before it reaches the ground."

Jack's board reached the ground wholly intact. To my surprise, Ernest shot just as well as Fritz in this event.

"There may be a time when ammunition fails, so you must also be adept at handling a bow and arrow."

To my great pleasure, my older boys were quite skillful. Even little Franz performed respectably.

After a rest period, there was a running match to Falconhurst.

"The first to bring me my penknife from my sleeping

room will be declared the winner of this event."

Fritz and Jack ran all out, taking the lead at once. Ernest started at a steady pace, and I predicted he would be more likely to maintain his pace than his brothers.

Before long, a galloping noise came from the bridge. Jack, astride his buffalo, was heading toward us with the onager and donkey following.

"Jack!" I scolded. "This is supposed to be a foot race!"

"I saw I hadn't a chance, so I made Storm gallop home with me in time to see the others come puffing in. These other two rascals followed uninvited."

Ernest was the race winner, having reached Falconhurst a full two minutes before Fritz. We then tested the climbing powers of the young athletes.

Jack was the champion climber. Riding followed that, with Jack and Fritz showing equal skills. Little Franz amused us by riding upon the back of Grumble, the young bull calf, and brandishing a whip.

Swimming concluded our island sports carnival. Fritz was a master. Ernest gave too much effort, Jack was too violent and hasty, and both grew exhausted quickly. Franz showed promise of future skill.

We returned to our dwelling where Elizabeth had gone earlier to prepare the awards ceremony. We found her seated with the prizes set out by her side.

For winning the shooting and swimming, Fritz received a double-barreled rifle and a beautiful hunting knife.

Ernest, winner of the running match, was given a handsome gold watch.

For climbing and riding, Jack was given a pair of silver-plated spurs and a riding whip.

Franz received a pair of stirrups and a driving whip made of rhinoceros hide. We hoped these would build in him the character of a bull trainer.

"That concludes our awards ceremony," my wife announced.

"I don't think so, Liz," I said, smiling. "There is one more award, for showing great talent in housekeeping, wifery, and motherhood."

Liz blushed happily when I handed her a workbox filled with every imaginable thing a lady needed for her worktable.

We then sat down to a late supper and afterward joined in family worship. Our Thanksgiving Day had been a great pleasure and success.

In the weeks after our celebration, I anticipated the arrival of the rains. I pressed forward with work to build our stores for the winter. We gathered roots, fruits, grains, potatoes, rice, guavas, sweet acorns, and pinecones. Load after load arrived at our cavern, and Mother's needle was active as the demands for more sacks and bags increased.

CHAPTER 7

The weather grew stormy and unsettled. Windy storms with thunder, lightning, and torrents of rain swept over from time to time. The sea water, hissing and foaming against the cliffs, signalled the approaching rains. It was near the beginning of June, and we had twelve weeks of bad weather waiting for us.

We established ourselves and some of the animals at the salt caves. The boys went to Falconhurst often to fetch anything we needed.

The darkness inside the cave annoyed me. Jack and I used a bamboo pole to hoist up a large ship's lantern. With its four wicks and large supply of oil, it gave a fair amount of light. Now, with better visibility, we spent several days arranging the salt cave's various rooms.

Ernest and Franz fixed shelves and set in order the books we had salvaged from the wreck. Jack and his mother took over the sitting room and kitchen, while Fritz and I, better suited for heavy work, arranged the workshop. We set the carpenter's bench, lathe, and large chest of tools in convenient places and hung many other smaller tools on the walls.

Those projects completed, we still found work to do, work necessary to maintain comfort and conveniences of life that at home we had accepted as everyday things. But I was glad for the work, the more the better. During our weeks of confinement, we needed ways to strengthen and maintain the health of mind and body.

We occasionally amused ourselves by opening chests and packages that had not yet been investigated. We found mirrors, clothes, a pair of tables with marble tops, various clocks, and a music box.

Our salt cavern was fitted up like a palace, and the boys begged me to settle on a name for our dwelling. After a little thought, I settled on Rockburg.

When the rains stopped and we were once again free to roam in the open air, we went for a walk along the coast. Fritz observed something on the small island near Flamingo Marsh.

The next day we made minor repairs to the boat, then set out to see what Fritz's discovery could be. It proved to be a huge, stranded whale. Before they were halfway to the monster, however, my boys were distracted by beautiful shells and coral branches they found.

"No doubt thousands of shellfish have been detached from their rocks," I explained, "and dashed in all directions by the waves, which have thrown ashore even such a huge creature as this whale yonder."

Looking the whale over from a distance, we decided to return later with tools to allow us to use the whale for oil and blubber. We gathered coral to take back with us this trip. Fritz wondered about the use of the coral.

"It is chiefly used to make beads for necklaces and things," I told him. "It is greatly prized by savages and might be useful in bartering should we fall in with any natives."

After hearing of the whale and the proposed work to be done in the afternoon, Franz and Elizabeth wanted to go with us. I consented but required we take along food, water, and a compass.

"The seas have just stopped raging," I explained. "We could still be detained on the island or forced to land quite a distance from home."

We could use a great amount of oil from the whale in the lantern that burned day and night in our cave, so we towed along all available casks and barrels. We also took along knives and hatchets. Our boat was so loaded the rowing was difficult and tiresome, and Fritz asked if I could possibly fashion some sort of rowing machine. I told him I would have to think on it.

My wife was startled by the size of the whale. I estimated its length at sixty-five feet, its width between thirty and forty feet, and its weight not less than fifty thousand pounds.

It was velvety and black, its eyes quite small, and its jaw opened to about sixteen feet in length. The tongue was soft and full of oil, as I had hoped.

We set about cutting slabs of blubber, again to provide oil. I also cut strips of the thick skin for use in making harnesses and other leatherwork.

We returned home to clean ourselves and decided to return to the whale at dawn the next day. I would split the carcass open and take out various portions of the intestines, thinking they would be fit vessels for holding the oil.

We worked all the next day, then left the remains to birds of prey and, with a full cargo, set sail for home. After a refreshing bath, clean clothes, and supper, we slept peacefully.

Next day, we heavily pressed the tubs of blubber, so the purest oil flowed into our waiting vessels. Then we boiled the blubber and strained it through a coarse cloth to obtain a supply of excellent train oil. The awful smell of this job offended us all, most especially my dear Elizabeth.

This project done, I set about making that rowing machine for the boat. Everyone wanted to give it a try when I was through, so we made plans to make trips to Cape Disappointment and Prospect Hill the next day.

We checked our little farm near Prospect Hill, obtaining coconuts and young plants along the way. The fowls were enticed by handfuls of grain and rice, and my wife caught as many as she wanted.

When dinnertime came, we dished out the whale's tongue, which had been cooked at the boys' request and to my great amusement. One after another, with dismal faces, they proclaimed it "awful stuff," begged for pickled herrings, and tossed the remainders to the dogs.

Elizabeth packed up everything while Fritz and I gathered sugarcane shoots, which I wished to plant. We then directed our course toward Whale Island, as we had named the place where we had found the beast.

On landing, I began to plant the saplings we had brought.

The boys helped for awhile, then went looking for coral and shells, leaving me and their mother to complete the work.

Jack came running back, shouting, "Father! Mother! I have found a skeleton of some fearful beast. A mammoth, I think!"

"Jack," I said, laughing at his youthful imagination and exaggeration, "have you forgotten our friend the whale?"

"No, Father, it's not the whale! This thing has huge beast bones instead of fish bones. The whale most likely floated out to sea. This mammoth is ever so much bigger! Come and see!"

We went to Jack's skeleton which, of course, proved to be the whale. Our footprints were on the ground, around the broken jaws where we had hacked out the whalebone.

"Still, Father," said Fritz, "it is a marvelous structure. Couldn't we use the bones for something?"

"Nothing strikes me now, Fritz, but we will leave them here to bleach awhile. Perhaps later, we could saw them up to make a few chairs, or a reading desk. But now it is time to return home."

A few days later, I was seated with Elizabeth and Fritz, engaged in wickerwork and chatting pleasantly, when Fritz rose suddenly.

"Father, I see something strange! First it seems drawn in coils on the ground, then rises as if it were a mast, then sinks and coils again. It's coming toward the bridge!"

My wife called the other boys and retreated into the cave, where I told them to keep watch with firearms at the upper windows.

I looked through the spyglass. "Just as I feared, an enormous serpent. We shall be in great danger, for it will most certainly cross the bridge."

Fritz asked if we could attack the monster. This would be impossible to do safely.

"Go up to your mother now and help load the arms. I will join you after I observe the monster's movements."

As the monster writhed and undulated across the bridge, I joined my family. Our hearts beat, and prayers whispered through our lips as it neared us.

One after another the boys fired, and even their mother discharged her gun. The shots had no effect. Fritz and I fired with steadier aim, and the monster entered the reedy marsh to the left and disappeared.

I had recognized it as a huge boa constrictor and advised no one leave the house without my consent. We waited for three days, and it did not reappear. But the restlessness of our geese and ducks told us it still lurked near.

We had to go for provisions. While we were preparing, Elizabeth opened the door, and Grizzle, our donkey, bounded out. Fritz would have run after him had I not held him back.

In horror, we watched the snake rear its head from the marsh, its dark and deadly jaws wide open. It wound around Grizzle, compressing him in order to swallow him.

We watched helplessly as the boa kneaded Grizzle into a shapeless mass. My wife, with Franz, found the scene too horrible and, trembling, hurried into the cave. The rest of us were fascinated by the dreadful sight.

This performance lasted from seven in the morning until noon. When the awkward morsel was finally swallowed, the serpent lay stiff and motionless. I felt this was the time for attack.

Fritz and I fired together, both balls entering the skull. We advanced closer and fired our pistols directly into the head. A quiver ran through its body, and the boa lay dead.

We raised a cry of victory. My wife approached cautiously, holding Franz tightly by the hand.

"I hope that terrible noise you just made was a signal of victory."

"See this dreadful creature dead at our feet? Let us thank God we have been able to destroy such an enemy."

"Amen," said my dear wife, gathering her boys around her.

CHAPTER 8

Following the gruesome death of Grizzle, the boys were not eager to accompany me to the marsh. Jack swore he had cold shivers each time he thought how his ribs could have been smashed by the snake's great tail. I did not yield to their reluctance, and we crossed the marsh by placing planks and wicker hurdles on the ground.

Beyond a thicket, we discovered a grotto of considerable size. The roof was covered with stalactites, and the floor was strewn with fine snow white earth that had a soft, soapy feeling.

"A pleasant discovery!" I exclaimed. "This is just as good as soap for washing. And it will keep me from having to boil soap."

Fritz and I went farther into the grotto to find a source of the soapy substance. I wished to gather a quantity to take home with us.

Emerging from the grotto again, Jack pointed us toward Ernest's location. I found him weaving a basket in which to catch a fish. He had shot a large eel, which now lay covered with rushes.

"This will make an excellent supper tonight, my boy. I am proud you had the courage to kill it, instead of running away in fear it may have been another boa!" I exclaimed.

Over the supper Ernest had provided, I discussed the importance of finding out if any other serpents lurked about.

"I want the entire family to go," I added. "Mother and Franz, too."

Because the expedition would take several weeks, we took a small tent and all sorts of provisions. We also toted along firearms, tools, cooking utensils, and torches.

The packed cart was hitched to Storm and Grumble. Jack and Franz mounted the animals and acted as riders and drivers. Elizabeth sat comfortably in the cart, Fritz rode ahead of the party, and Ernest and I walked. The dogs and Fawn, our tame jackal, flanked us.

Heading toward Woodlands, we saw traces of the serpent's approach to Rockburg. We stopped briefly at Falconhurst and were welcomed by the poultry, sheep, and goats there.

When we arrived at Woodlands at nightfall, all was peaceful, with no signs of the boa. The little farm and its inhabitants had flourished.

Next day, taking Juno's pups, Fang and Bruno, we surveyed the immediate neighborhood. There was a great rustling in the thicket. Franz fired, and I heard him happily cry:

"I've hit him!"

"Hit what?"

"A wild pig! And bigger than Fritz's!"

Examining its webbed feet and unusual teeth, I decided it was a capybara, a water-loving animal of South America.

We opened and cleaned the carcass to make it lighter and

easier to carry, then put it in a game bag. Franz carried it himself until he was quite tired. We then strapped it to Bruno's back and soon reached Woodlands again.

The next day's journey took us near the Gap, where we had once made an arbor of the branches of trees. Instead of pitching the tent, we spread a sailcloth over the top of the arbor. It made comfortable quarters for the short time we would stay there.

We found no trace of the boa, or any of its kindred, in the canebrake. It had been awhile since we'd enjoyed the juice of these canes, so we refreshed ourselves.

One day, we took a short trip to the farm at Prospect Hill and found that vagabond apes had wrought terrible mischief there. The animals and poultry were scattered, and everything in the cottage so torn and dirtied, there was no hope of clearing it up that day.

"We'll return at a later time," I said to my rather downcast family.

Several days later we crossed a stream, which we had named East River, and we paused to fill our flasks with water. It was good we had done so because, continuing our journey, we soon appeared to be surrounded by a desert.

We proceeded slowly, the boys grumbling uncomplimentary remarks about the "new country" under their breath the whole time.

"Arabia Petrea," groaned one. "Desert of Sahara," sighed another. "Fit abode for demons," muttered another.

"Patience, Boys! I am certain we will soon find water, fresh grass, trees, and a nice place to rest."

We came to an overhanging rock. There we rested under its shade and had refreshments.

After our hunger had been subdued and our weariness somewhat abated, Fritz looked out over the plain before us. After a moment, he exclaimed, "Either my eyes deceive me, or there is a party of horsemen heading toward us. Could they be wild Arabs of the desert?"

"Certainly not!" I said. "But take the spyglass, for we should be always on our guard."

The spyglass was passed from hand to hand. When my turn came, I saw the members of the herd coming toward us were very large ostriches.

"We must try to catch one," I said, excited. The feathers alone are worth having."

The boys, of course, were much more interested in the prospect of riding on the back of one than in having its plumes as a treasure.

As the five ostriches drew near, I saw through the glass that only one was male. He was beautiful, with the white plumes of his wings and tail contrasting nicely with the glossy black of his neck and body.

Catching one would not be easy. When pursued, ostriches run for hours in a wide circle. The hunter generally gallops in a much smaller circle, waiting to attack until the bird is tired.

"They use their powerful legs as weapons," I told the

boys. "They will kick forward and cause great injury to dogs and people, if attacked without caution."

We took position and held the dogs concealed as much as possible. But they grew impatient and struggled from our grasp. Before we could reach the spot, the dogs had torn up the flesh of the male. Its splendid plumes were marred by blood.

"What a shame we couldn't have caught him alive," said Fritz. "I'm sure he would have stood over six feet tall."

As we stood looking at the sad sight, Jack ran toward us, shouting and waving his cap.

"I wonder what that boy has found now," I said to his brothers.

"Eggs, Father! A whole nestful of ostrich eggs!"

We followed him to the spot and found a nest of more than twenty eggs, each as large as an infant's head. The thought of taking more than two with us was ridiculous, but the boys would have liked to clear the nest.

"We will make a landmark, I promised them, "So it will be easier for us to find the nest again."

We took two eggs with us and continued on until we found a marshy place with a brook. We sat there and again took some food.

We resumed our journey and found a charming valley shaded by clumps of graceful trees. We agreed to call the place Glen Verdant.

Ernest went a little ways ahead of our group with the dogs. We lost sight of him for several moments, then there arose a cry of terror, violent barking, and surly growls. We rushed forward, and Ernest met us, looking white and shaken, out of breath from running.

"Father, a bear is coming after me!"

An enormous bear appeared, followed by another. Fritz and I leveled our guns and fired together. We hit them, but they were only injured. One had a broken lower jaw, and the other took a bullet in his shoulder and was somewhat lamed.

We advanced with loaded pistols. I shot one through the head, and Fritz shot one in the heart as it reared up to spring on him.

"Thank our good Lord!" I cried as the beasts sank to the ground.

While we had not found serpents, we had certainly rid ourselves of equal dangers. We dragged the bears to their den, so we could return later and have ourselves a couple of splendid bearskin rugs and meat for several suppers. We also hid the ostrich eggs in a sandy hole and left them behind, planning to return later to fetch them.

We reached the tent by sunset. Franz and Liz had prepared us a hearty meal, as well as a tidy watch fire.

It took us two days to scrape, wash, salt, and cleanse the bearskins. We were glad of this occupation during the tedious process of smoking the bears' meat.

We still had leisure time, and the boys grew so weary of inactivity that I gave them permission to make an excursion alone.

"I prefer to stay here, Father," said Ernest. "I would like to make some ornamental cups from the ostrich eggs."

"Very well," said I.

Franz wanted to go, and, having left the invitation open to all, I could not refuse him. They were well armed, well mounted, and committed to the care of Fritz.

"Look up to your older brother and obey him," I instructed. "Godspeed and bless you, my dear boys!"

Those of us who stayed behind passed the time in a variety of useful occupations.

Evening approached. The bears' paws, stewing for supper, gave off pleasant and savory odors. We sat talking around the fire and listened for sounds announcing the return of our young explorers.

What funny looking figures returned to us! Franz and Jack each had a young goat slung on his back; the four legs, tied together, stuck out under their chins.

Fritz's game bag looked rather odd. Round lumps, sharp points, and occasional movements seemed to indicate life within.

"Nothing like real hunting," cried Jack.

"Fritz has two angora rabbits in his bag, and we brought you some honey."

"My brothers forget the chief thing," said Fritz, proudly.

He went on to explain that they had driven a small herd of antelopes into our territory.

"They are there," he continued, "for us to hunt or to catch

and tame at our leisure."

"A job well done! But to your mother and me, the chief thing is that God's goodness has brought you safely back to us."

We all then sat around while the boys gave us details of their excursion. Mother summoned us to dinner, then we lit our watch fire and all slept soundly after a day of hard work and adventure.

Next day, we did manage to trap a rather obstinate ostrich. Using strong cord, we made him march between Storm and Grumble and headed for our home at Rockburg.

Late one evening, Jack came thundering along on the back of the ostrich we had tamed, with Fritz and Franz following in the distance. Fritz and Franz toted along their bulging game bags, the contents of which they emptied. Four birds, a kangaroo, twenty muskrats, a monkey, two hares, and half a dozen beaver rats were proudly laid before me.

"Oh, Father!" Jack exclaimed. "Riding on an ostrich is such fun. And we go so fast! You really must make me a mask with glass eyes for riding, or one of these days I'll be blinded by flying debris."

"Ha!" I replied. "I'll do no such thing!"

"Why not?" he asked, amazed.

"First, I am the adult here and do not feel I must do anything you demand. Second, you are quite capable of doing it yourself."

I congratulated them on their supply of game and had them look after their animals. We then enjoyed the appetizing meal Liz had set before us.

The time for our first grain harvest neared, and the amount of work before us startled my wife. Harvesting would add reaping and threshing to the chores of fishing, salting, pickling, and other daily chores we already had.

"But with all this, what will happen to my manioc roots and potatoes?"

"There's no hurry on the manioc, and digging potatoes in this soft ground is a sight easier than in Switzerland. And we shouldn't need to plant more if we leave the young plants in the ground."

Without further delay, I leveled a space of firm ground to use as a threshing floor. It was well-sprinkled with water, rolled, beaten, and stamped. As the sun dried it, it was watered again. This process continued until it was as flat, hard, and smooth as a threshing floor needs to be.

We slung our largest wicker basket between Storm and Grumble, armed ourselves with reaping hooks, and went to gather the wheat in the simplest, quickest way we could.

"Boys, don't worry about the length of the straw. Just grasp the wheat where it's convenient for you, so you won't tire too quickly from too much stooping."

Each boy was to wind a stalk around his handful and toss it onto the basket. In just a short time, the basket had been filled many times, and the field was a display of tall, headless stubble.

The sheaves were placed in a large circle on the threshing

floor. The boys mounted Storm, Grumble, Lightfoot, and Hurricane and went round and round, trampling and stamping the grain, while puffy clouds of dust and chaff flew around them.

When our harvest stores were finally housed, we were delighted to find that we had reaped sixty—eighty—even a hundredfold what had been sown.

I changed the crops in the field to rye, barley, and oats.

"Well, Liz," I said to my wife, "I just hope they ripen before the rainy season."

She nodded. "But for now," she said, "I believe we should thank our Lord for allowing us to make a reasonable life here."

We all knelt in prayer.

CHAPTER 9

Ten years passed by on this island, and the story was chronicled in the pages of my journal. Shades of sadness at the thought of the steadfast passing of time were overshadowed by thoughts of gratitude to God for the safety of my family, and for my sons reaching manhood as strong individuals.

We had settled on New Switzerland as the name of our island. Rockburg and Falconhurst continued to be our winter and summer homes. Shark Island, now clothed with graceful palms, guarded the entrance to Safety Bay. The swamp was now a lovely lake, with just enough marsh and reeds to form good cover for the waterfowl for which it was a favorite retreat. On the lake sailed blacks swans, white geese, and richly colored ducks, and among the water plants could occasionally be seen marsh fowl, cranes, herons, and flamingos.

The farm at Woodlands flourished. Our flocks and herds supplied us with mutton, beef, and veal. My wife's dairy was almost more than she could handle.

We had been blessed with good health these years, though Elizabeth occasionally suffered from light attacks of fever, and the boys sometimes met with minor accidents.

Fritz was now twenty-five, of moderate height, strong, active, muscular, and high-spirited. Ernest, twenty-three, was tall and slight. Mild, calm, and studious, he had refined tastes and great intellectual power. Jack, at twenty, resembled Fritz, though lighter built. His grace and agility were greater than his muscular strength. Franz, no longer a child at seventeen, had some of the qualities of each of his brothers. He was witty and shrewd.

They were all honorable, God-fearing young men. They were dutiful and affectionate toward me and their mother and warmly attached to one another.

"I have been considering," I said to my wife, "that our Fritz is of an age to be dependent upon himself. Therefore, he is given the liberty to take any excursions or voyages alone, without fear of alarming us should he remain absent longer than we expected."

Fritz looked gratefully toward me. His mother embraced him. "God bless and preserve thee, my boy!"

Fritz set off on his own the next day. When missed by his brothers, I explained he had gone off to explore more of the coast. "If he finds it interesting," I told them, "he may be gone two or three days instead of a few hours."

I didn't express any suspicion, any hope that he would find other human inhabitants.

Fritz was gone five days. I could not conceal my anxiety, and we all went to look for him. En route, we came across a canoe driven by a dark, swarthy native. I hoisted the white flag and took up the speaking trumpet. I spoke as many peaceful words from the Malay language as I could recall. This produced no effect, and Jack grew impatient, taking the trumpet from me.

"Come onboard, you chicken, and make friends, or we'll blow you and your—"

"Stop, you foolish boy! You will alarm the man with your loud words and wild gestures!"

"But see, Father, he is paddling toward us!"

The blackened wastrel turned out to be our own Fritz, in disguise! He came aboard, assailed by hugs, kisses, and questions.

Fritz told us of his adventures and discoveries. I asked if he knew of a good anchorage for the yacht. He said he could lead us to an island where we could anchor the yacht. His glance at me was full of meaning as he returned to his canoe and led on to his island.

Following Fritz on the island, we emerged from a thicket and saw before us a hut of sheltering boughs. At its entrance burned a cheerful fire. In a moment, Fritz came leading by the hand a slight, handsome youth, dressed like an English naval officer.

"This is Edward Montrose," he introduced his companion. "Will you welcome him as a friend and brother into our family?"

"That we will, indeed!" I exclaimed, holding out my hands to the younger stranger. "Our wild life may have roughened our looks and manners, but certainly it has not hardened our hearts!"

Elizabeth and I had to conceal our amusement, for we could both see quite clearly that the youth was a girl. I could see by the expression on Fritz's face, though, that she wished this to remain a secret until Elizabeth could find her more appropriate clothing. My other boys were so happy to see another human being that they didn't seem to notice.

Fritz was the one who let the cat out of the bag, by referring to her as "Miss Montrose." He endured a few minutes of good-natured teasing by his brothers. When the confusion died down, he told us how he had found Miss Montrose. He had found a rather tame albatross carrying this note: "Save an unfortunate Englishwoman from the smoking rock!"

Fritz had returned a message to acknowledge receiving hers, and his excursion had taken him in search of the "unfortunate Englishwoman." When he found her, she hurried toward him and warmly grasped his hands.

"Long, long I have waited since the bird returned with your message," she exclaimed. "Thanks to God, you have come at last!"

I was less interested in their meeting than in exactly who Miss Montrose was and how she came to be here.

"Jenny, Father," said Fritz. "Her name is Jenny."

"Jenny, then," I smiled. "Let us hear where this child of God has come from."

She was born in India where her father, a British officer, had served many years. Her mother had died when Jenny was just three. Under her father's guidance, by the time she was seventeen, she was as much at home on her horse in the field as she was in her father's fine drawing room.

"Then my father received orders to return home with his troops. He did not want me to accompany him in the ship with the troops. He put me aboard the *Dorcas,* due to sail for England the same time as his ship."

Jenny's ship had met a storm, and she and the crew were obliged to take to the boats. After enduring the perilous sea for days, they sighted land. The other boats had disappeared, but those on Jenny's attempted to land. The boat capsized, and Jenny alone had made it to shore.

We had all listened attentively, but now we were tired. Fritz retired to his kayak, the boys and I to the deck of the yacht, and Elizabeth and Jenny to the shelter.

Next day we went to Falconhurst. After working there for a week, we returned to Rockburg. Winter would soon be upon us again.

CHAPTER 10

Jenny and the boys took turns telling or reading wondrous tales as we sat drawing and weaving in our cozy study. It was the happiest winter we had ever spent.

The rain ceased, and we were called to activity once again. We men attended to the field, garden, and orchard; Elizabeth and Jenny found abundant occupation in the poultry yard and house.

One evening, our work done, Jack and Franz loaded an empty tub into the kayak and paddled it out to sea, as a mark for practice. They rowed a little away and fired. The barrel flew to pieces. They gave a shout of triumph and cleaned their guns.

Then, as if in answer, three shots boomed across the water from the west. We were speechless. Had the boys fired again? No! They were hastily paddling toward us. They had heard the sound, too.

A tumult of feelings—anxiety, joy, hope, doubt, and fear—rushed through our minds. Was it a European ship that would return us to civilized life? Or was it Malay pirates, who would rob and murder us?

"Oh, Fritz," said Franz, joining us on shore. "It must be a European ship. We shall see our Fatherland again!"

All eyes turned to me. Night was drawing and, at present,

we could do nothing. What would I advise? "We must make what preparations we can today, then pray for guidance."

Few of us slept that night. We took turns keeping watch from the veranda, in case more signals were fired, or a hostile visit was paid to us.

About midnight, a fierce storm brewed. The hurricane raged for two days and two nights. Then, on the third day, the sun appeared and the wind and sea calmed.

We went to Shark Island to discharge our guns. One. . . two. . .we fired and waited. It took a few minutes, but an answer finally rolled in the distance. We returned to shore to find the family quite excited.

Fritz and I armed ourselves with guns, took a spyglass, and paddled the kayak out of the bay and round the high cliffs to our left. In a little sheltered cove beyond the cape lay an anchored brig with English colors at her masthead.

With my glass, I could see several figures on deck, several tents pitched on the shore, and the smoke of fires rising among them. Fritz took the glass from me.

"I can see the captain, Father. He is English, I am certain!"

We watched a few minutes longer and assured ourselves the brig would be there a few days. I wanted to appear to these strangers in more dignified a manner. We wanted to pay our respects to the captain, not as poor shipwrecked creatures begging assistance, but as masters of the land seeking the purpose of the strangers visiting the coast.

We spent the rest of the day preparing our dainty craft.

Her decks were scrubbed, her brass guns polished, and the English flag hoisted. Mother overhauled our wardrobes, and our neatest uniforms were made ready.

Next morning, we set out for the brig, carrying baskets of fruit as presents for the strangers. The others waited on our yacht while Fritz and I went aboard the brig. The British captain cordially welcomed us. He led us to his cabin and asked how he had the good fortune to be visited by residents of a coast thought uninhabited.

I gave him a brief account of how we arrived here. I also told him of Miss Montrose and how Fritz had rescued her from her lonely position.

"Then," he said, rising to shake Fritz's hand, "let me thank you in the name of Colonel Montrose."

He explained that, though three years had passed, the colonel had never given up hope of seeing his daughter again. He went on to say that he had run across three men who declared themselves survivors from *Dorcas*.

"I obtained permission to cruise these latitudes, hoping to find further traces of the crew. My efforts have been rewarded by unlooked-for success."

The captain then begged to be introduced to my wife and Miss Montrose. One of his officers was dispatched with a yacht and a polite message, and Elizabeth, Jenny, and the rest of the boys were soon aboard.

At luncheon, the captain told us he had an invalid aboard, a Mr. Wolston, with his wife and two daughters. The voyage had been recommended for his health but had not done as much good as anticipated. Tents had been pitched on shore so the family could rest.

We met Mr. Wolston and his family that afternoon. His family were delighted to see us and were such agreeable company that in the evening we were still upon the shore. It was too late to return to Rockburg, and the captain kindly offered us tent accommodations.

That night, Elizabeth and I had a serious talk as to whether we really wished to return to Europe. At first, neither of us seemed eager to say our true feelings, afraid they might be different from the other's. But it soon became clear neither of us had a desire to leave our beloved New Switzerland.

"I do require, however, that two of our boys remain with us," she said. "The other two must promise to send us a good class of emigrants to join us and form a prosperous new colony."

"Yes, but which two shall stay?"

She thought a moment. "That, we shall leave up to them."

I agreed and planned to consult with Captain Littlestone on the subject of placing our island under the protection of Great Britain.

CHAPTER 11

At breakfast the next morning, we proposed that Captain Littlestone bring his ship to Safety Bay, where we could enjoy a visit at Rockburg. I thought perhaps Mr. Wolston might benefit from the comfortable residence on shore.

My boys planned a marvelous welcome for our visitors. An eleven-gun salute greeted them. The royal standard of England floated majestically on the morning breeze.

Mr. Wolston was carried ashore and established in my room. A camp bed was added for Mrs. Wolston, so that she might conveniently attend her husband.

Toward evening, Mr. Wolston asked if it was agreeable that he and his wife, with their eldest daughter, make a long stay on the island. Their younger daughter, for the present, would go to her brother at the Cape of Good Hope.

"Should we decide to stay permanently," he added, "I would suggest that my son leave the Cape and join the colony."

We welcomed his proposal with sincere satisfaction and told him of our wish to stay the rest of our days in New Switzerland.

"Hurrah for New Switzerland!" I shouted.

"New Switzerland forever!" shouted the rest. We raised our water glasses and made them touch with a musical ring.

"Prosperity to New Switzerland! Long may she flourish!" echoed all around.

"Long life and happiness to those who make New Switzerland their home!" Ernest said.

"Won't someone wish the same for those who go away?" asked Jenny. "Much as I wish to return to my father in England, my decision will waver if all the cheers are for New Switzerland."

"Three cheers for England and Colonel Montrose!" Fritz cried. "Success and happiness to those of us who return to Europe!"

"Well," I said, when silence was finally restored. "Since Fritz will return to England, he must bring happiness to a mourning father by returning to him this dear daughter, whom I have already begun to think of as my own."

"I promise, Father."

Ernest had chosen to remain with us on New Switzerland, and Elizabeth and I had promised him any scientific appointments we could manage.

"And what is Jack's choice?"

"I wish to remain here." He chuckled a little. "I stand in awe of European schools and fear I'll find myself caught and pushed into one should I stand too near."

"A good school is what I dream of," said Franz. "There, I have a chance of rising in the world. Fritz may someday return here, but it might be well for one of us to go home with the intention of remaining there forever. I am the youngest and could more easily adapt than the rest to a different life. My dear father, however, will decide for me."

"You may go, dear son," I replied. "God bless all our plans and resolutions. The whole earth is the Lord's, and where, as in His sight, you lead good and useful lives, there is your home."

I asked Captain Littlestone if he was able to carry out the wishes of those who chose to leave.

"My orders were to search for a shipwrecked crew. Survivors from two wrecks have been found. I am most willing to take those who wish to return into my care. Every circumstance has been wonderfully ordered and linked together by Divine Providence, and if England gains another colony, it will prove a fitting addition to this fortunate chain of events. Three cheers for New Switzerland!"

Our emotions ran deep as the party separated for the night. Some felt they were standing on the threshold of a new life. I felt a weight roll away from my heart and thanked God that a difficulty which, for years, had given me anxiety was now solved.

Captain Littlestone allowed us as much time for preparation as he could afford. Still it was short, so the settlement was a bustle of activity for several days.

We packed up anything that would add to our children's comfort on the voyage or benefit them on their arrival in England. A large share of my pearls, corals, furs, spices, and other valuables were added to give them a good position in the world of commerce.

I gave them private papers, money, and jewels that had been the property of the captain of our ill-fated craft and asked them to hand them over, if possible, to his heirs. A short account of the wreck, including a list of the names of the crew I had found, was given to Captain Littlestone.

Fritz, having already told me of his affection for Jenny, was advised to ask Colonel Montrose to sanction their engagement. I gladly bestowed my consent, as did his mother, who loved the sweet girl dearly and heartily grieved to part with her.

The evening before our separation, I gave Fritz the journal in which I had chronicled the events of the shipwreck and our life, asking that he make every attempt to have it published.

"As you know," I said, "it was written for the instruction and amusement of you boys. However, it is possible that it may be useful to other young people. Children are very much alike everywhere, and you four lads represent the lot of them who are growing up in all directions. It will make me happy to think my journal may lead some of them to observe how blessed are the results of patient continuance in well-doing, what benefits arise from application of knowledge and science. And, most importantly, how good and pleasant a thing it is when brethren live together in unity, under the eyes of paternal and godly love."

It is night. For the last time, my united family members sleep near my care.

Tomorrow this closing chapter of my journal will pass into the hands of Fritz, my eldest son. From afar, I greet thee, Europe! Hail to thee, dear old Switzerland!

Like thee, may New Switzerland flourish and prosper—good, happy, free, and thankful to God!

If you enjoyed

CHRISTIAN ADVENTURES,

check out these other great
Backpack Books!

GIRLS' CLASSICS
Including *Pocahontas,
Little Women,
Pollyanna,* and *Heidi*

GOD'S AMBASSADORS
Including *Hudson Taylor,
David Livingstone, Gladys
Aylward,* and *Jim Elliot*

BIBLE HEROES
Including *Noah, Joseph,
David,* and *Daniel*

AMERICAN HEROES
Including
*Roger Williams,
Abraham Lincoln,
Harriet Tubman,*
and *Clara Barton*

BIBLE HEROINES
Including *Deborah, Ruth,
Esther,* and *Mary*

MODERN HEROES
Including *Corrie ten Boom,
Eric Liddell, Billy Graham,*
and *Luis Palau*

THE SON OF GOD
Including *Jesus,
The Miracles of Jesus,
The Parables of Jesus,*
and *The Twelve Disciples*

Great reading at a great price—only $3.97 each!

Available wherever books are sold.
Or order from
Barbour Publishing, Inc.
P.O. Box 719
Uhrichsville, Ohio 44683

If ordering by mail,
please add $2.00 to your order for shipping and handling.
Prices are subject to change without notice.